Lessons From A Dog Guide

Sermons On The Second Readings For Sundays In Lent And Easter

Dallas A. Brauninger

CSS Publishing Company, Lima, Ohio

Copyright © 2003 by
CSS Publishing Company, Inc.
Lima, Ohio

Scripture quotations unless marked otherwise are from the *New Revised Standard Version of the Bible*, copyright 1989 by the Division of Christian Education of the National Council of the Churches of Christ in the USA. Used by permission.

For more information about CSS Publishing Company resources, visit our website at www.csspub.com or e-mail us at custserv@csspub.com or call (800) 241-4056.

ISBN 0-7880-1985-6   PRINTED IN U.S.A.

To Bob, speaker of gentle words

Table Of Contents

Introduction

I am not usually a great enthusiast for a series of lessons for any liturgical season. My mind is easily distracted and doesn't seem to be able to capture the rhythm and flow that the author intends. This was not the case with Dee Brauninger's "Lessons From A Dog Guide." I had, and I am sure, will have over and over again, a wonderful time reading her work.

Dee's writing ministry is such a gift. She has a way with words that makes one's heart sing and be open to learn and hear more. As I was reading I kept calling out to my spouse, "Listen, listen to this...." Gentle phrases leap out and make one think and wrestle with God and one's self.

Dee and dog guides, Dolley and Treasure, help all of us understand that God chooses unique ways to reach us. Dee, Dolley, and Treasure and the ancient, ever-powerful words of scripture help us begin to understand that our faith is living and growing. Our faith "reflects a partnership of patience and acceptance, a team effort between God and the human family."

It is this team effort, so wonderfully illustrated with story, that pushes me to places that I am normally afraid to look, let alone dare experience. Dee's words open my eyes to see that asking for help is a gift, not a failing, and that trust can be experienced even under the toughest conditions. She also brings my euphoria of newly learned truths down with the bump of "Finding one's self is not necessarily permanent." There will always be work to be done. The good news is that none of us have to do the work alone — God and dog guides and good friends and strangers will be there.

I took my position as the Inclusive Ministry Coordinator to work with various marginalized folks in our church and the world. I hope to help our church be faithfully hospitable to everyone. I hope to be able to give strength to others as we work for justice and shalom. The incalculable gift I receive daily from my position is the friendships, helpful hints, confrontations about my "I'll do it alone" attitude, and strength to know that I am not alone — God and others are with me. "Lessons From A Dog Guide" is the perfect companion piece to help me into the rhythm and flow of partnership. I believe that you, too, will find joy and courage, hope and deep meaning in this delightful collection of sermons.

The Rev. Margaret Slater,
Inclusive Ministry Coordinator
The United Church of Christ
Cleveland, Ohio

Preface

Years ago, having visited with a woman with multiple sclerosis who worked with an assist dog, I replaced the phone receiver with a sense of awe. The dog's presence enhanced this woman's physical stability, enabling her to leave behind walker and wheelchair for periods of time. At a curb, it lifted by her pant leg the foot that could not rise by itself. The dog then positioned her foot on the sidewalk. Bracing herself against the dog's shoulders, the woman brought the other leg to the curb.

Indoors, the dog nudged her body into a sitting position so she could rise from her bed. The woman could place a shirt on her head but lacked the strength to pull it on or remove it. The dog took care of that, too. Further, it turned door knobs, but it refused to open an outside door when it perceived the woman was having a difficult day.

I marveled but grasped neither the depth of this team's communication nor the breadth of her assist dog's training and skill until seventeen years ago when I became part of an assist dog team. I soon became aware that in addition to guiding my path, two successive dog guides also quietly offered nonverbal guidance that nurtured my faith. Each guide embodied singular attributes that responded to troublesome phases of my life. When I struggled with self-acceptance, a dog guide was provided that excelled in unconditional love. When impatience was the difficulty, the dog guide modeled patience.

Moreover, these dogs appeared to convey to parishioners a truth about the journey into hope that words sometimes fail to express: Let hope get inside of you and let yourself move inside of hope, the metaphor of dog guide said.

When we speak about God's presence, who is to say where in the hierarchy of spirit the line is among God, the human family, and an animal called dog? Sometimes, particularly when we resist the usual forms, God chooses a unique way to reach us. Sometimes, God offers a dog guide to teach a sense of team, trust, steadfastness, or perseverance. Perhaps of fullest impact, this helper has taught a greater understanding of oneness of spirit, that all things are related.

These Lenten/Eastertide lectionary-based scriptures lend themselves to the metaphor of a dog guide team. Our faith, also, is more than unquestioning trust. It grows by bits and pieces. It reflects a partnership of patience and acceptance, a team effort between God and the human family.

It may be that something within the telling of this collection of lessons from a dog guide will conjoin the metaphorical truths of the book of Revelation with the practical religion of the Apostle Paul. Paul wants to wake us up to ourselves. He returns us to the every day of practicing our faith. Revelation is the reward for having done the work of Lent. The message of Revelation says, also, I hear the note of your ongoing struggle. This struggle need not drown out the exquisite music of your life. I sing a song of courage and hope.

Ash Wednesday
2 Corinthians 5:20b—6:10

The Ash Connection

There is always something we cannot stand about ourselves, something that is unacceptable, something that has reduced us to ashes. There is always some need for us to be reconciled to God. There is always a chance for us to become reconciled to ourselves.

On Ash Wednesday, we become aware of the ashes of aborted plans, miscarried hope, and infertile dreams — the ashes of having fallen short. We are vulnerable and needy. We need to bring these ashes to God so God can blow them away to reveal to us a new creation. We need to set aside a time to come back home to ourselves.

The setting aside time of the Lenten season, beginning with Ash Wednesday, is an acceptable time for us to speak to God and for God to listen to us. However, before renewed life can happen, we must become ready.

Once there was a dog guide team. The actual assist dog changed from time to time as the years passed and the dog retired. As time went on, the dog's blind partner grew in team skill, gaining many lessons from her dog guides. The initial lesson, however, taught the woman about being ready. When she was ready, having done the prework, she found that opportunity for the next step would present itself to her.

To observers in their small town, it appeared that the dog guide located buildings by magic. Indeed, the dog did guide its partner from their house to a shop downtown after only a two-word command.

First, however, the woman had to determine the route to the shop. Then, using a series of commands, she gave the dog guide block by block instructions until they arrived at the store. Upon reaching their destination, the dog guide received an identifying word — Safeway. From that time, whenever it was told to find Safeway, the dog required no further instruction.

Becoming successful as a dog guide user necessitates another type of prework. The dog/person team must establish a close relationship. It is helpful, first, for dog users to have come home to the reality of their blindness. Then they can embrace with whole heart the hope of a good working relationship with their dog guides.

A college student who returned to the dog guide training facility within a year for his third replacement dog discovered the impact on his dogs of his inability to accept his blindness. He would continue to have unfortunate experiences with dog guides until he came to terms with his blindness.

Having perceived the student's anger, his first dog had destroyed the man's dorm bed mattress. His second dog became aggressive with other students. The acceptable time of readiness for an honest dog/person work bond would arrive only after the man came home to himself.

The bonding of another dog guide team was immediate. A blind pastor did not know what to expect from her first assist dog. While visiting with a suffering parishioner, the pastor herself was overcome with emotion. Perceiving her feelings, this compassionate dog rose and approached the minister. With profound gentleness, it slowly washed the tears from her face. At that moment, the woman trusted the team to work. Her working dog possessed the unteachable capacity to blow away ashes and extend her human partner's freedom.

Let us view Ash Wednesday ashes now from the perspective of the tangible black stuff from fireplaces that gardeners welcome. Ash feeds the plants of thriving vegetable gardens. An essential nutrient, potash or potassium promotes both healthy stems and plant roots. It improves fruit production. From the ash in the soil, potassium makes its way into cherry tomatoes, snow peas, and other garden produce.

This transformed ash moves on to renew the cells and muscles of the human family and to help maintain the electrical stability of the cells of the human heart and our nervous system. This high source of potassium is the same wood ash that some church folk will use on this day to mark the cross of Lent on their foreheads.

What does all this talk about workable dog guide teams, coming home to ourselves, and a well-fertilized garden have to do with the beginning of the Lenten season? The variety of ash in our lives draws us to a fuller sense of the connectedness of all things.

Consider the symbolism in the natural world of a growing seedling that became first a tree and then the Good Friday cross. Later it might have been burned for fuel and returned to ash. Eventually, it may have re-entered the soil to nourish a new sapling.

Or, let your heart be drawn to the tree that was a palm and whose branches were strewn in honor on the path, the green carpet that Jesus would follow into Jerusalem on Palm Sunday. Perhaps you placed in a special spot in your sitting room a dried palm frond from Palm Sunday a year ago. Today, you might have burnt it to the ash daubed on your forehead in the shape of a cross to remind you of Jesus' death and resurrection.

Or, consider the phoenix of Egyptian, Russian, Chinese, and Japanese mythology. The large, gentle bird that is said to live from 500 to more than 12,000 years self-combusts, burning to ashes. After three days, this symbol of rebirth and life after death is renewed. The phoenix rises to new life from its ashes.

Let us review also the following signs of renewed life:

- The transformation that a dog guide brings to the uneasy mobility of one who does not see.
- The thick, renewed growth that sprouts from the ashes of a great fire at Yellowstone National Park.
- The resilient human spirit of determination and concern for oneness of people worldwide that rose from foot upon foot and yard upon yard of ash sludge at the World Trade Center site.

Consider in our lives any journey from life to death to renewed life and the hope that ascends from ash of despair at the acceptable time. Consider the fresh start, the new creation, that comes into our being at the right time. Consider, amid the ashes, the discovery that we are fully alive. We who, like the people of old Corinth, thought we had nothing, in fact possess everything.

Hear anew the Apostle Paul telling us of God's promise, "At an acceptable time I have listened to you, and on a day of salvation I have helped you" (v. 2). Hear the charge to come back home to ourselves. Hear the beckoning to move toward the new creation of reconciliation with ourselves, with God and Christ. (See 2 Corinthians 5:16-20.) Now is the time our hearts can become ready to hear the words from Revelation as words for us, that God stands ready to listen to us and to wipe away our tears of suffering. (See Revelation 7:17.)

As we move through this time of coming back home, let us notice the curious placement of pre-Easter scripture. These passages offer us segments of Second Lesson letters to the Corinthians, Romans, Philippians, and Hebrews. These selections draw us toward two queries: How best can we use Lent as a time to acknowledge suffering? Why is Lent the time to put suffering into perspective? These Lenten texts lead us toward a greater reality of how things are with us so that on Easter morning we will be able to hear for ourselves God's promise of hope.

After Easter Sunday, in case we did not get it the first time, we will spend several weeks with the book of Revelation. This book of the Bible offers a journey through the metaphorical expression of Lent reflection and Easter promise. Ascension Sunday returns us to Paul with his note to the Ephesians.

When is the acceptable time to ask God to listen to us? When is the acceptable time for God to bring help? Such questions rise from within the chaos of suffering and wondering if God has deserted us altogether.

Does this acceptable time depend in part upon when we are open to accept it? Is making ourselves ready a prerequisite? Do we have to wait until when the acceptable time has come for God to be ready? Drawing upon similar words from the Hebrew prophet Isaiah (49:8), Paul reminds us that now is the acceptable time: "For he says, 'At an acceptable time I have listened to you, and on a day of salvation I have helped you.' See, now is the acceptable time; see, now is the day of salvation!" (v. 2).

14

Now is the time for our hearts, yours and mine, to become ready to hear the words from Isaiah to 2 Corinthians to Revelation as words for us. God stands ready to listen to us and to wipe away tears of suffering. (See Revelation 7:17.) This holy now can come at any time because of the promise by God that the God of grace is by our side.

Incarnation With A Wagging Tail

Once there was a dog guide named Leader Dog Dolley. Dolley was a cross between a golden retriever and a German shepherd.

"Dolley," her human partner said, "soft, gentle, free-spirited dog guide, you take the fear out of my blindness. Your nose presses warning against my shin. I feel your head checking to the left then to the right. Your harness jiggles loosely in my hand. That means you are in the 'Leader Position.' I feel the muscles of your body and you tune into mine. We work as one.

"Most of the time, Leader Dog youngster, you remember to wait for me at a street crossing. You check my foot position before we negotiate a curb together. We feel its depth with unison stride. Sometimes, Dolley, your exuberance to show me you know the way overpowers your Dolley Madison dignity.

"Dog guide, you prance with pride yet match the varying paces of my arthritic body. Teammate of only seven weeks, how can you know me so well? Our instructors said a good match is vital. They worked for eighteen months with you. But how, Dolley girl, how could they have gleaned from a written application the strength of my spirit? How did they find a match for my sense of joy? How do you know me so well?

"My lifemate says you look at your harness hanging in the hall then wag your tail in anticipation. I agree, Dolley. I will match your determination. I will do your skill justice.

"You love to be on a mission, to go somewhere with a purpose. I tell you, Dolley, I know where I want to go. You do the looking. This is our charge: You find the way. I promise to yield my struggle

17

for total independence. Together, we will have courage. Together, we will gain freedom.

"Hello, Dolley. Hello, tomorrow."

The relationship of the whole human family with God resembles the unique partnership of an assist dog team. A dog guide does not care that its partner cannot see. It asks no questions. It imposes no conditions beyond trust. It neither bullies nor demeans. Rather, it responds with its whole, joyful heart and with its whole, skillful being to the human need it perceives.

Sometimes, providing precisely what we need, God comes to us in an unusual manner. Rather than dispatch a negative focus upon the deficits of our being, God begins at the starting point of who we are in reality. God sees both our potential and our wholeness without diminishing us because of our shortfalls. No matter how we are or who we are, if any one among us calls to God with whole heart and whole being, God answers with quiet, joyful acceptance.

In these next weeks, we shall journey through the soul-sharing relationship of a blind friend and her assist dog. Let us reflect upon what this journey says to the inner passage that you and I have chosen to resume during these Lenten days.

What does the word of faith say to us? How do we believe? Heart to heart? Is that not what our religion is, a heart to heart relationship?

Ours is not a distant religion on a long, loose leash but an accessible faith as firm as the hand on the sturdy harness of a dependable dog guide. Ours is not a long-distance faith but is rather like a cellular phone conversation with God that we can engage in at any time, from any place, and for any reason.

The level of trust requisite to a fruitful working partnership with a dog guide is analogous to a generative relationship with a generous God. Neither is easy, yet both are simple.

The leap into the unknowns about faith calls for courage. The background fear of doubt is always ready to assert itself. However, the exhilaration of realizing that in God's perception we are essentially valid and worthy persons braces our effort. Our growing sense of admiration and our growing sense of respect jumpstart Easter joy.

From within this mystery of understanding and being understood, a root of mutual responsibility begins to thrive. It pushes through fertile soil. This new partnership cancels the isolation of whatever disabling condition of body, mind, or spirit has deterred our going forward. No longer alone in the business of marking time until some dreaded end, we gain a renewed sense of hope.

Why is it so hard? Why is it so hard to have faith and then, once we have it, to allow faith of sufficient strength that we can keep it to gain a hold on us? The Apostle Paul understood about faith. "The word (that is, the word of faith that we proclaim) is near you, on your lips and in your heart," Paul told the church at Rome (v. 8).

Why is faith so hard if it is so near that it is all but palpable?

Why does it take so much, first of all, to admit and confess that one needs a dog guide to find the way? More than needs, it requires this partnership for a life with quality.

Why does it take so much initially to entrust to the discretion of another of God's creatures the safety of one's life?

Why does it take so much before the joy of discovering the new freedom and the regained self-respect from being so gently, carefully, and devotedly attended to comes tumbling in?

The answer lies in the little word, "If." Paul tells us, "If." "[I]f you confess with your lips that Jesus is Lord and believe in your heart that God raised him from the dead, you will be saved" (v. 9).

"If" is not an if only or a wish to or a just do it. "If" is the hinge word that implies a matter of choice. "If" tells us we must become involved before it can happen. "If" says it is waiting for us to take the next move, if ... then. In the case of faith, "if" is a high-pressure word with a low-threat result.

To Paul's thinking, the "if" of faith has two canons: Confess with your lips; believe in your heart. It takes both believing and confessing to contain the mystery of faith. Faith needs both solitude and a listener. We need solitude for our own pondering. We need the presence of God and other persons to hear us and give an object to what we say.

Which comes first, believing or confessing? In one verse, Paul mentions believing first. In the next, he says confessing first. Believing and confessing go hand in hand. We need the solitary stuff of the inner heart from which belief and hope grow. Yet believing somehow does not become real until we know the freedom of speaking aloud to someone else what we believe.

If we approach faith from the other direction and confess first, that is, acknowledge belief that something is true, this telling somehow strengthens that belief. This is the mystery of faith — the letting go of doubt while embracing that doubt, the encircling of uncertainty with a hug of possibility, the yielding while heralding, "Okay, God."

Paul says believing with our heart that God raised Christ from the dead is what justifies us. Justification is the act of being freed by God both from the guilt and from the penalty of having caused grief or pain or anguish to another.

The apostle says confessing with the mouth that Jesus is Savior is what saves us. Salvation frees us from the power of sin and evil. It saves us from the destructive force within us that causes harm and frees us for hope. Our action is belief and confession. God's action is justification and salvation.

What we want and hope to do is to believe the Resurrection story is more than a theory. We cannot know absolutely because we do not contain that wisdom. We do know that when human hope evaporates, God always surprises us by leading the way ahead with new hope. When God perceives that we are ready, God responds with a joyous heart. We do not know how hope happens, but we have a clue from a dog guide, an offered, given, and ready symbol of possibility who delights in freeing its partner for hope.

God is God who looks out for us, all of us. God, the same God of everyone, will save all who call on God in the name of God. No wonder the end note of the first Sunday of this Lenten journey is a song of joy.

High-tension Wire

A two-lane state highway bisects the little town of Hemingford in western Nebraska. Highway 2 is not one-sixteenth as congested as I-80 before a Big Red football game. Nevertheless, the highway is busy.

In that part of the state, prairie winds often throw the sound of an approaching vehicle. This makes it difficult for a person who does not see to determine by ear the approximate distance and speed of the vehicle.

On their own, early in the first week home after training school, Dee and Leader Dog Dolley prepared to cross Highway 2. Her hand on the handle of the dog guide's harness, the woman said the "Forward" command at the curb. This position rendered the dog guide the responsibility for the woman's life.

Just as they reached the crown of the road, Dee heard a vehicle approaching with considerable speed from her right. The direction of the wind had blocked its voice until the farm truck was almost upon them.

Too scared to rush forward but unable yet to entrust full control to her dog guide, she returned responsibility to herself. She did not give the new dog guide a chance to do its work. She dropped the harness and held only the dog's leash. "Around! Around!" she shouted. Pivoting on square, they raced back to the curb.

The woman dropped to the ground. She wrapped her arms around the dog. "I'm sorry. I won't do that again," she said. "Now let's do this over. This time, Dolley, you be in charge."

Her task was to trust her dog guide with her life. The time to start trusting was now. Otherwise, she might as well turn in the dog guide along with her freedom.

One evening not long afterward, it was the dog's turn to be spooked. Apparently not seeing well in the twilight, Dolley refused to pass by a large garbage container set out near a sidewalk they had traveled over only hours before.

The dog guide, also, had to overcome fear before she could carry out her work. Dee worked her repeatedly from the cross curb. Each time, they crept closer to the refuse container. After each attempt, she praised the dog for being brave until the grand rejoicing when Dolley passed by the container without hesitation. Having seen each other's vulnerability and shared each other's humiliation, the dog guide and the woman began what would become a decade of trusting and assisting each other. Each refused to give up on the other because of shortcomings. They gained enough internal strength to proceed with the quiet, intelligent confidence of a mature guide dog team.

Honesty of working together to avoid being overcome by fear builds any team, not just a dog guide team. With or without a disability, discouragement occurs with the day-to-day of living. Standing firm brings the steadiness of spirit that allows us to concentrate on making progress. Considerable gaining of heart happens whenever we adopt an attitude of determination. We meet with decision whatever changes come into our lives.

At times, blindness is like the benign center line of a highway that suddenly becomes a high-tension wire. It takes both the dog guide and the human being working together to neutralize the threat of adverse conditions.

Strength also requires gaining the capacity to show our fear to those whom we trust. When it comes to fear, everyone has a choice. When life scares us, we can curl into a ball like a poked slug, or we can give a good stretch and proceed forward.

Every time a person with faulty or absent sight steps outdoors, that step requires having made the choice of courage over fear. Every time any person with a special need moves beyond the known or the comfortable, there is opportunity to meet courage. At the rise of each day, first thing, make a choice. We either meet the morning with apprehension or greet it with courage.

From time to time, a blind person who uses an assist dog is asked if it is not a humiliating sign of weakness to be led around by a dog. The response of choice is not that of degradation but of freedom. This tethering is not an affront. It is an honor.

Courage in any circumstance never comes with ease, but a courageous spirit is contagious. By the time you and I know courage, we also know humiliation and vulnerability. Vulnerability is somewhat self-imposed by the limiting or handicapping dimensions of a disability. Humiliation is somewhat other-imposed by attitudes of society in general and by those specific persons who contribute to feeling that one is a lesser person.

Again, humiliation and vulnerability are not exclusive to those with physical disability. Any special need of body, relationship, economics, or spirit can spawn similar trouble. Courage can nullify feelings of humiliation and vulnerability here, too.

By living the day-to-day of our lives as Christians, we stage a study in the quiet tenacity of persistent courage. Vulnerability is also part of the "body of our humiliation" of which Paul speaks in verse 21. This vulnerability speaks of our lack of capacity to give in to temptation, to the negative energy of others, or to anything else that distracts us from the goal of being strong in faith.

Paul has a way of needling us into the reality of how we live out this faith. The troublesome "we/they" dichotomy of being a Christian dissolves. The familiar holier-than-thou attitude disappears when we acknowledge that within each of us live at least a few undesirable "they" elements. We are as vulnerable to these humiliations of body and spirit as the most artless Christian or any other member of the human family.

Paul offers an antidote of courage for us, as he does for the people of the church in Philippi. He shows considerable passion for these early Christians. He addresses them with warmth, as people "whom I love and long for, my joy and crown ... my beloved" (from v. 1). His goal for them is to avoid defeating the higher ends to which a Christian aspires by stumbling over lesser focus "on earthly things" (v. 19b).

Special to each of us is an extensive list of these "earthly things" that compete for our energy. Paul says this god "is the belly" (v. 20). Furthermore, in addition to ignoring the negative dimensions of such a life, we have fun engaging in many activities of the belly. When earthly things prevail, we waste on this negative stuff the positive effort we might have expended on standing firm. Let us, Paul might say, decide upon what we plan to stay focused.

Addressing the Philippian church with the earnestness of intimacy, the apostle urges these folk to "stand firm in the Lord" (v. 1). Standing firm is difficult. Standing firm requires that we contact the core of courage available within us, and that requires having enough self-compassion to give ourselves a chance.

Speak not only of isolated incidents of courageous action. Even a hearty burst of courage will dissipate after its moment. Our need for courage is ongoing. Courage is a chosen way, an attitude of response. Stand firm.

Despite all effort to plant ourselves with resolve and to refuse to compromise, we still need something beyond ourselves. While our standing firm seems a solitary thing, it needs grounding in our relationship with God.

When the prairie winds of the soul threaten to skew our perception, we must keep in mind that one from another realm keeps our direction steady. One who knows the Lenten struggle of courage and who quells the taste of fear stands with us, stands ready, and stands steady. We call this one Christ.

Paul says, "Brothers and sisters, join in imitating me, and observe those who live according to the example you have in us" (v. 17). Let us seek our models and mentors, those from history and those in our present surroundings. Among these models of single-minded persistence are Paul and Christ.

Paul's call to us is to stand firm, but stand firm in Christ. As we see throughout Lent and Holy Week, Christ will let nothing deflect him from his course or garble his purpose. The transforming capacity of Christ which awakens our capacity of transformation is our saving grace. This is the holy glue that adheres hope to purpose.

When our faith grows fragile, God, we need someone stronger to urge us forward. Bring into our hearts the living models of those who have been faithful to you.

When we lose hold of hope, God, we need a measure of courage. Send us renewal of hope in whatever traditional or unparalleled form will stir our boldness.

Remind us always that Christ is Christ. Amen.

Moment By Moment

The Christmas-Easter-only people do have a point. Those who arrive at church only at Christmas and Easter somehow must know deep inside that participation in communal worship is a necessity. It is a prerequisite for survival. Granted, they miss a lot in between. However, let us merit the coming. They appear not just for show. They come out not solely because of the family dinner after church.

Something greater calls to them at Christmas and at Easter. Something within wants to hear it again. Something needs the reaffirmation that God is with us always and that God will be with us always.

The "they" is also the "we." We regular churchgoers also switch off worship sometimes, coming only in a state of inattention, except at Christmas and Easter. The story is still the same old, old story, but somehow we, also, hear it anew.

Each successive year, you and I have trudged our way through many changes. As did the people of Paul's Corinth, we need to hear again that no testing will overtake us that is not common to everyone. We yearn to hear again that God is faithful, that God will not let us be tested beyond our strength.

The gap between Easter and Christmas is too great to wait for such fortification. When we miss a Sunday, we easily slip out of hope's rhythm. We need reassurance that with any testing, God will also provide the way out so that we may be sustained in our journey.

27

Who has not spoken or heard these words, "God will not give you more than you can handle"? In our helplessness to say anything else were we the speakers of such words, we may have jumped to them as a handy bromide. Were we the hearers, we might have thought, "Oh, really, and how do you know?"

We may wonder if testing is a prerequisite to everything. This query that slips into our thoughts must have occurred also to the people of Paul's time.

Let us backtrack. When Paul lectures the Christians at Corinth, he sounds like a frustrated parent who lets go with a string of lambasting at a recalcitrant child. Then with negative energy expended, the tone of voice gentles to notes of compassion and encouragement.

Throughout the first ten chapters of Paul's first letter to the Corinthian church, the apostle responds to news that its members have been squabbling and strutting and competing with one another. Human vanity could have spawned this turmoil. The tension of constant pressure to be the church in difficult times could be the culprit. Whatever was going on, Paul wanted to avoid coddling this church.

He had to call this fold to careful, persistent discipleship. They should not turn things around and grump at God. They are not to test God. They are not the first group whose faith has been tested. When the grumbles take over and you feel as if you were being singled out for abuse, he says, you are not. Paul takes them back to the Hebrews whose faith also was exercised. He warns the Corinthian Christians about becoming mighty and high. They, too, will trip. Testing is a continual part of the commitment.

Then, reminiscent of the Hebrew prophets, Paul softens. He says, "No testing has overtaken you that is not common to everyone. God is faithful, and [God] will not let you be tested beyond your strength, but with the testing [God] will also provide the way out so that you may be able to endure it" (1 Corinthians 10:13).

Dee's dog guides had provided the way out so that she could move beyond enduring living nonvisually to regain her sense of wholeness. One frigid December, her second dog guide experienced a two-week downtime due to a bout of cold-triggered arthritis.

28

The woman realized then that in her mind she already had programmed the dog guide to work at least ten years, the length of her first dog guide's career. When despair burst out over the possibility of an aborted work life of this assist dog after only five years, she needed quiet words from her husband to return her focus to hope. He said, "You just have to let Treasure be himself."

Something about his words scattered the negative energy that had overtaken her spirit. After all, both dog guides had taught her that it was okay for her just to let her be herself.

Assisted by a human guide, she walked the short distance to the gathering room in the church where she would take her morning walk for the next two weeks. Toward the end of that time, Treasure became well enough to lead her to the church. However, he chose to lie on a sunny spot on the carpet while she designed configurations around the eight long tables.

As the dog's body discomfort subsided, he began to accompany her around the room. His endurance grew. The morning he refused to enter the church. she knew he was well. The team resumed its usual outdoor walking pattern.

Whatever the difficulty, it is easy to lose heart. A businessman has had continual reversals in his financial and work life. A young man who suffers from a complicated brain disorder finds himself in a frequent chaos that disrupts his entire being. The condition will be with him the rest of his life.

If only, we say, an ailment would be acute for once so we could just get it over with. The chronic conditions in our lives and those of the world stay with us. Whatever the anguish, it takes experience to gain trust that feeling lost within is not necessarily permanent. It takes experience to realize that neither is finding one's self necessarily permanent.

I spoke recently with a woman who had been tutoring a young man who lives with a perceptual difficulty called dyslexia. He had made a false start in college and lost his confidence. The woman reported that after several weeks of tutoring, the man had passed the re-entry tests and was readmitted to the college. The tutor and her student decided, however, to continue their sessions. The woman said, "We must help each other on the journey, or some will never make it."

When I asked what had helped this young man the most, she said, first, it was encouraging him to spot the moments of hope. Whenever he noticed that he was on the upswing, they would celebrate the possible. He had begun to learn that celebration of the possible still can have the edge over defeat.

Second, he began to redefine testing as a time to focus on his capacity. He began to anticipate finding solutions rather than slumping under the weight of testing as an enemy of progress.

How beautiful it is to see those we care about work hard to greet who they are in the light of hope. Whether age 19 or 45 or 87, life may carry hardship, but celebration of the possible still has the edge.

I once asked a woman whose body is besieged by advanced rheumatoid arthritis how her spirit has managed to survive. She said that when she understood being free of discomfort was no longer a reality, she began paying attention to the little breathers, some as brief as few moments, that came during the day. She came not only to count on and cherish these brief pauses in the pain but also to recognize them as a gift, a way out that God provides.

God may be telling us in many ways to practice being people who avoid slewing onto the path of living on the defensive. Rather, let us choose to concentrate on greeting the continual testings that come our way with as positive a problem-solving attitude as we can muster. This stance also is a response to God's call to careful, persistent discipleship.

Whatever the situation, whenever we see that we are on the upswing and whenever we begin to celebrate that gain, however minute or for however short a time, this is the time to say, "Yes, I will remember this. I will remember that I am capable of thriving because God provides a way out of the jumble."

When we can recall the treasurable experience of having been lost and being found, we can strengthen our trust that we can come through the journey regardless of how often the prodigal, the illness, the inability, or the loss shows itself. Then we can practice celebrating the possible.

Salvation's From And For

Despite the zest to adapt when things go amiss with the human body or the mind, a self-alienation and sense of being unacceptable can ooze into our spirit. Part of this self-disliking grows from the disappointment of lost dreams that precedes the discovery of a new purpose. The nerve-wrack of frustration with societal and physical barriers incites estrangement from ourselves. The need to find other ways to manage spawns some of the I-am-not-okay in anyone who encounters a significant change.

Did you know that for the nonvisual person, a user-friendly cellular phone costs five times more than a standard one? The adapter that enables a nonvisual diabetic to use a monitor for blood glucose levels carries an even more outrageous price tag.

Anger with the cost of time, money shortage, and lengthening list of tools necessary to function also contributes. The normal grieving process of loss undercuts joy and causes a once-fervent sense of expectation to sag.

With words from her song, "Into the Dark," youth artist Anna Hill sings, "When my lights are out/I can't see my way/The darkness so overwhelming/I long for the light of day...."[1] Then at the critical moment, along came an assuming four-pawed creature called a dog guide who wheedled her way into the scowl and turned everything around.

From the beginning of their team, Leader Dog Dolley endorsed her partner's validity with vigor. Her every action spoke:

"You are acceptable to me. I love you."

"Go ahead and be who you are. I love you."

"I love you as you are, therefore, you will be able to love yourself again and to accept yourself as you are. I love you."

"I will neither let go of you nor will I desert you on your journey. I love you."

The strength of these clear, nonverbal messages gave the human partner of Leader Dog Dolley the permission to be who she is. As far as Dee was concerned, God had sent a dog guide with this dog's particular qualities at the right time. The woman began to comprehend at the level of soul the kindness of an incarnate God.

She revived her created self, the person she recognized. She again practiced the art of "I can." The dog persisted. Day after day, Dolley worked her guiding work with Dee as if blindness were nothing out of the ordinary. Dolley's unconditional love and open acceptance were at once antidote for the venom of self-loathing and vaccine against unacceptability. In becoming teammate with this once-dejected woman, the dog guide transformed a solitary journey into one within community.

This is what reconciliation is about. We bring ourselves to accept. We settle some inner argument that had suggested the broken parts within us cause us to be broken and unworthy people.

As we become reconciled to ourselves, the reestablishment of the inner friendship draws our focus outward toward harmony with God and toward reunion with those around us. Reconciliation presupposes a previous relationship. Reconciliation also notices that the relationship is salvageable.

Here God enters the drama of reconciliation. One may think resolution of dis-ease is a one-person enterprise, but people motivate each other to reach for survival. We also need the intervention of God. Simply put: why does such a closeness grow between a nonvisual person and a dog guide? Absolute necessity for survival. And why does such a closeness grow with God? Absolute necessity for survival.

Reconciliation is difficult. Reconciliation must be from God. It must be a ministry. Reconciliation is effortful, if not impossible, for us to reconcile ourselves by ourselves.

The starting point of our ministry of reconciliation is our perception. "From now on, therefore," Paul tells the Corinthians, "we regard no one from a human point of view; even though we once knew Christ from a human point of view, we know him no longer in that way" (v. 16).

If we are no longer to regard anyone from a human point of view, then you and I will see ourselves and others with different eyes. Perhaps Paul means with these words that we must try to look at others through God's eyes.

Paul might mean also that we are to look for the presence of God in each person we encounter. Think about that. What would happen in the evolution of human relationships were we to look first for God's presence in an individual or within ourselves? Paul might suggest further that we, as God does, see and accept the whole person, human frailties and all.

In today's passage, Paul speaks about God's hand in saving us from ourselves. Paul talks about God's saving us for ourselves. Paul mentions reconciliation five times. First, he says that God "reconciled us to himself through Christ" (v. 18a). Then he says that God "has given us the ministry of reconciliation" (v. 18b).

"That is," Paul explains further, "in Christ God was reconciling the world to himself, not counting their trespasses against them" (v. 19a). Paul then tells us that God's reconciling us to himself through Christ also meant God's "entrusting the message of reconciliation to us" (v. 19b). God saves us not only from ourselves but for others.

Finally, Paul urges and "entreats [us] on behalf of Christ, [to] be reconciled to God" because "we are ambassadors for Christ, since God is making his appeal through us" (v. 21). Rather than reconcile the people of the world to each other, which is the task of the people of the world to work out, Christ reconciled the world to himself. We have been entrusted with the message of reconciliation as ambassadors, but this way of serving is given within this frame of reference: the way of Christ.

"So if anyone is in Christ," Paul tells us, "there is a new creation: everything old has passed away; see, everything has become new!" (v. 17). To reconcile brings us to a new place. Reconciliation countenances a moving on. We are always moving on, not back. We cannot return to Genesis chapter 1 because life changes us. Instead, as we discover that reconciliation is the rebirth of hope, we move on to a new genesis, that of a new beginning.

God continually makes all things new. God's continually making all things new has everything to do with bringing us to this new place in our lives. When God reconciles, God reunites our whole creation to its creator. When we involve ourselves in a ministry of reconciliation, we return the world to God's self.

Reconciliation is not in isolation but is also a saving for. A sense of purpose emerges. Paul phrases this purpose as our being "ambassadors for Christ." God has given us an assignment. We are to be Christ's ambassadors. That will call for a few changes in how we live. Better get ready. This assignment tells us that God/Christ needs us to carry out God's design for unity among neighbors down the hall, across the street, and across the ocean.

The Christ dimension that we take on in becoming ambassadors for Christ makes all the difference. It is our nature to tally up our own trespasses and those of others all the time. Christ, God, asks us to forgive others their errors. What a huge difference exists between our smallness of heart and the generosity of Christ's heart.

This is the difference that being in relationship with Christ makes. In spite of everything, God is continually making all things new. This reconciliation has little to do with changing what cannot be changed, what is aged and worn out, or what is broken about us. We can become new despite the giving out of mind, body, or spirit.

In the beginning, in the middle, and at the end of all this, God is still God who still cares deeply about us, deeply enough to save us from ourselves, deeply enough to save us for ourselves so that we might serve others. In the words, again, of songwriter Anna Hill, "One light shining in this dark place/Makes a world of difference, leaving its trace."[2]

---

1. Lyrics and music by Anna Hill, member of the Christian rock musical group, Outspoken, from Friend, Nebraska. Copyright for "Into the Dark" held by the composer. Used by permission.

2. Bridge from "Into the Dark" by Anna Hill.

Season Of Beginnings

Tangerine peelings and coffee grounds,
Peanut shells and faded daffodils,
Exhausted green pepper and tomato plants,
Pungent, black clumps of grass clippings,
Brown leaves from a sycamore tree.

A compost pile is a gathering place of discarded living matter that has lost its usefulness, its flavor, and its purpose. With a layer of microbe-rich soil, a measure of aged farm manure, and a little moisture, the pile's cooking and blending season begins.

As each ingredient loses its identity, the compost pile shrinks until tangerine peelings, grass clippings, and used up plants have changed into a uniformly textured black soil-like substance. The finished compost is ready to begin its next season of life as high-energy nourishment for a new crop of garden plants. Lent is the season for gathering up and discarding whatever has lost its usefulness, its flavor, and its purpose in our lives.

The Japanese people greet every new year with an immaculate house. In our country, there was a tradition before there became no time for it where every household underwent a thorough housecleaning each autumn and spring I once knew a woman who cleaned her closets on occasions of needed emotional housecleaning. Whenever she found herself drawn to this tedious task, she knew her inner self was asking for contemplation time. It was time to let go of something no longer useful to her emotional health.

Lent is the season for cleansing the soul's house. Lent is the season to begin such letting go.

Dee spent nine months of gestation and many tearful nights before she could release Leader Dog Dolley after a decade of service. The letting go began with the arthritic dog guide's retirement from active work. Strolling through their yard after traveling together one sunny afternoon, Dee removed the dog guide's work harness and lengthened her off-duty leash. "Now, Dolley," Dee said, "find your favorite spot in the grass."

"Now, lie down and roll in the grass," she said. As the dog stretched her back in the soft turf, Dee told her, "Dolley, this is retirement."

In the next days, whenever they returned home from working, Dolley nudged her toward the grassy spot. The arthritic dog was ready to retire. To avoid breaking Dolley's heart, Dee eased the dog into her husband's care. When the dog could endure the separation of a closed door, she forgave Dee's words, "I'm safe, I have my cane. Take a few minutes off."

The dog watched through a window as her partner used her mobility cane to travel the length of the driveway to the mailbox. Later, always telling Dolley where she was going, the woman walked out of the dog's sight the two blocks to the grocer. Eventually, she could stretch her absence to a three-hour separation.

Both the dog and the woman were able to accept the new dog guide that shared their lives for several months before Dolley was put down. To avoid confusion, Dee no longer invited the retired dog guide to wear her work harness, but Dolley accompanied the new working team on leash for slow, short walks. Dolley had time to be a regular dog, spending as long as she chose in the summertime shade beneath a green cart.

When it was time for the final walk to the veterinarian, Dee drew the dog's work harness from the hall closet. With characteristic joy for her work, Dolley poked her nose through the harness and guided her person with Leader Dog joy for one last time.

Lent is the season for negotiating necessary transitions. Lent is the season for beginning to say the good-byes that will enable us to speak hello with a grateful heart.

A young boy often rode with his dad to the shore of Lake Michigan to watch the sun setting across the big lake. As parent and child sat together listening to the lap of waves and studying the clouds for first tinges of color, questions would take shape. Where does the sun go when it drops beyond the far side of the water? To begin a new day somewhere. What is over there on the other side of Lake Michigan? Wisconsin.

Lent is the season for pondering the mystery of life here and the mystery of life after here. Even though we can neither see nor define it, we can nurture the trust that continuing life will be. This is the season that we invite ourselves to touch into the area of the unknown.

Lent is a story about death and endings. Lent is a story about life and beginnings. This journey toward death and new life is planted within us from the beginning. Whether we admit it or not, perhaps we all become preoccupied with it at times. Is that why we yearn for Easter? During Lent we run our uncertainties, our curiosity, our dying, our perspective on loss, and our hope through the filter of Easter.

The Apostle Paul also appears to understand the struggle of letting go. Listen to the tension twinge as he speaks to the leaders of the Philippian church. Actualizing set goals is not easy. Admitting that he himself also is by no means perfect in accomplishing his goals, Paul says, "This one thing I do: forgetting what lies behind and straining forward to what lies ahead, I press on toward the goal for the prize of the heavenly call of God in Christ Jesus" (vv. 13b, 14). We can hear the intensity of Paul's words, his "pressing on" and his "straining forward."

Paul's personal goal is to know the power of Christ's resurrection. Paul seems at first to knock himself down for his incapacity to become as like Jesus in his death as he wants. Paul minimizes his own efforts. "Yet whatever gains I had," he says, "these I have come to regard as loss because of Christ" (v. 7).

Listen to the private longing in your own heart as it echoes the depth of yearning and passion in Paul's wistful confession. Paul says, "I want to know Christ and the power of his resurrection and the sharing of his sufferings by becoming like him in his death"

(v. 10). How immediately he draws us in. We also know such feelings. We, too, are imperfect, very human beings.

What is a productive way to share Christ's suffering today? How can we get closer to Christ by becoming like him in his death? Is this ancient or is it not so stale martyr talk that easily can become confused with unhealthy choices?

Some Christians take on a symbolic suffering throughout the season of Lent in order to experience the sacrificial suffering of Christ. Giving up sweets or meat appears at first to be at best only an annoying reminder of Lent, a weak imitation of sacrifice.

When things are going well, death matters usually are far removed from our minds. On the other hand, we each carry our own bag of sorrows that we wish were a sieve. But all is not always well. The "will it never end" syndrome appears when people know a great suffering. Those caught in the various concentration camps of spiritual or physical cancers need not practice sacrifice during Lent. They live it. The still bruising memory of a September Philadelphia flight makes a token sacrifice seem petty. Too much real stuff of suffering that life circumstances have forced us to give up makes the thought of serious deprivation unpalatable. We hunger for healing rather than more trouble.

Rather, let us try to take on a new goal of living quality during the final weeks of this Lenten season. Using the life of Christ as the framework to collect and surround our actions, let us exercise an extra measure of compassion in the family. Upgrade reading material and television viewing. Practice kindness in the workplace or at school. Set aside a piece of time for giving to others.

Paul tells us to forget the past. Let go of the past. Move forward. We can refine the meaning of present day practice of Lenten sacrifice by recognizing that Lent is the season for each of us to ask these questions:

What part of the past do we want to carry with us to cherish?

How do we determine what we need to leave behind?

Can we leave behind what is unfinished?

Can we decide to carry what is unfinished in a pocket then pull it out during those times we find ourselves strong enough or ready to look at it one more time before letting it go?

Are we willing to risk taking steps toward forgetting what is finished on the chance that we might move forward to what lies ahead with greater enthusiasm than strain?

Lent is the season for gathering up and discarding whatever has lost its usefulness, its flavor, and its purpose in our lives. With the energy and strength we have gained from this fruitful season, let us try letting go and moving on.

In Tandem

Have you ever ridden a bicycle built for two? When most of us think of something in tandem, we picture a tandem bicycle. This bicycle has two tires, two seats, and two sets of pedals — one set in front and one in back. It also has two pairs of handlebars; however, the rear handlebars, for support only, are stationary.

In addition to establishing an attitude of trust, two bikers operating a tandem bike need to work together. They must be obedient to a common goal. If the person in front tries to pedal while the one in the rear is braking, the bike does not move. When they find a rhythm of pedaling and lean together as a single unit, their combined energy can propel the bike long distances with relative ease.

Like tandem bikers, a dog guide and its human partner are connected mechanically. The connection of the person's hand on the handle of the rigid harness allows both the dog and the person to perceive and respond to each other's smallest movement. While this constant, mutual tethering at first might seem a potential enslavement, it extends the freedom of each partner by sharing their abilities.

When a young dog guide named Roselie led her blind partner down 78 flights of stairs to safety, the team worked in tandem obedience. Considering that these were the stairwells of the World Trade Center, filled with fumes from jet fuel and packed with scared people, we understand that dog guide was tuned to an additional obedience, that of dedication.

Christ lived in tandem with God. Like Abraham before him, who was willing to sacrifice his son Isaac rather than be unfaithful

41

to God, Christ also showed total obedience to God. He found the courage to face death rather than to let down God. God substituted a ram for Isaac, but God would not bring a lamb to stand in for his own son.

One day, when Leader Dog Dolley and her partner went to the hospital to visit a man who was nearing death, Dee witnessed her dog guide's capacity to connect soul to soul with a human being. As they left the elevator, the dog spotted the man's aged father sitting in the waiting room. Dolley led the minister over to him.

The dog must have sensed Hans' sorrow for she laid her chin on his knee. Hans took the dog's face between his hands and for several minutes accepted her loving gift without a word. Later, he said Dolley's eyes poured into his eyes the silent understanding and compassion she was so good at.

Sensitivity to a mutual awareness is part of a team's discipline. Dog guide users are taught to practice "dog-awareness." For effective dog management, no matter what else the person is doing, the partner also must stay connected emotionally with the dog.

Dog-awareness is like the parent who, while speaking on the phone, keeps track of a young child. Like children who sense when a care giver has forgotten about them, the dog, who perceives when the dog-awareness of its partner lapses, may begin to stray.

In time, Dee realized she and her dog guide shared a further refinement of this connection, that of being of the same mind. While the human partner was practicing dog-awareness, the dog guide exercised "person-awareness." They had become tethered in spirit. This obedience would bring them an even greater freedom and purpose.

Dee focused her attention on another person while working at her profession, but she also practiced careful dog-awareness. Sensing this, her dog guide soon learned to share her with the people who needed her. It was a subtle release, a "Don't be concerned about me. I'll be right here if you need me. You do your thing" permission.

Her second dog guide, Leader Dog Treasure, excelled at this dimension of their teamwork. Involved in conversation, Kathy and Dee sat in opposite chairs. Treasure lay at his partner's feet. When

42

it was time for a prayer, Dee took Kathy's hands in hers. As they reached forward toward each other and Dee began to pray, Treasure observed the change. He nosed his way into the circle their hands made. Throughout the prayer, he sat with his rump to Kathy and his head facing his partner as if he, too, wanted to receive the prayer.

Other-awareness, respecting another's freedom, voluntary obedience, and the discipline of caring all call us toward a greater sense of being with each other. They bring us to a fuller understanding of oneness with all of creation.

Passion Sunday calls us to human compassion. Compassion is the capacity to walk in tandem with another in a rhythm of quiet listening that transmits understanding of the heart. Such a connecting of spirit can enable a shared blossoming of spiritual energy without overpowering either person.

How rare is the finding of a soul mate, one we recognize to be of the same mind of which Paul spoke to the Philippians. If you have ever been around someone whose presence invites a loosening of your tongue, you may have found yourself speaking without reservation. Abandoning self-censure, you spoke with a sense of safeness and of being heard. How grateful and how freeing it is to be one in spirit. Such obedience to the greater-than-either-one alone focuses the sense of purpose and meaning of each one.

Paul draws us toward this higher compassion in his letter to Philippian church folk. Well-named, Passion Sunday is charged with feeling. On this Sunday that begins the final week of Jesus' earthly life, Paul's words invite us to let the same mind be in us that was in Christ. We see in him a voluntary obedience. Jesus was in tandem with compassion.

Jesus exemplified a unique power. His power lay not in an escape from being ordinary. His might was in an extraordinary journey that reflected the fullness of being an ordinary person.

When someone comes into power, we expect the ego of that leader to be noisy and strong, not humble. Christ asked no one to bow to him. With powerful people, we accept overstatements of self-confidence that ward off uncertainty. We do not anticipate from those in power a voluntary emptying of the self.

We expect that at the last minute those whose lives are in jeopardy will exploit all available clout and devise all variations of the power play, not disregard them. That explains the therefore of verse 9, "Therefore God also highly exalted him and gave him the name that is above every name."

So great upon us is the impact of Christ's sacrifice that at the mention of his name, something melts within us. The knee of our soul bends in confession and affirmation. When Jesus was afraid as well as at ordinary times, he remembered God-awareness. Because of God-awareness, Jesus gained strength and courage. God and Christ were of the same mind. They lived in tandem.

Lent has been the time to school ourselves in "being of the same mind" as Christ. How can we translate this obedience into a discipline that we can tolerate, follow, and obey today? How can we become soul mates with God?

Those who stood by the side of the road that first Palm Sunday must have thought it as impossible to maintain faithfulness as one in spirit, in intention, and in goals as we do today. This is why on this day of remembering Jesus' journey into Jerusalem, we too stand by the side of the road in awe of him.

So that we can begin to comprehend the incongruity of emotions on Passion Sunday, let us leave this place today with the invitation to ask a question during the pregnancy of significant actions in our lives this week. To what higher goal am I choosing to be obedient? Perhaps then we might come an inch closer to meeting God's person-awareness of us with our God-awareness.

Good Friday
Hebrews 10:16-25

In A Land Of Faithfulness

Good Friday is about faithfulness that happens because of forgiveness. You and I constantly need forgiveness because we constantly fall short. We remember our sins with such clarity that it is difficult for us to consider that, as soon as we speak of them with true regret to God, God no longer remembers our sins.

If the Israelis and the Palestinians would just forgive each other, a blanket of forgiveness might thaw the lifetime cycle of revenge and warm a spirited coexistence. Forgiveness lets go of the grudge. Forgiveness decides to lay aside the bad memories. Forgiveness lives within the category of the holy.

We wonder and we ponder how we can bring about a peaceful spirit among people who are addicted to upheaval. One answer rises from a passage within today's scripture. The author of the letter to the Hebrews writes: "Where there is forgiveness of [sins and lawless deeds], there is no longer any offering for sin" (v. 18).

Through the tenacious efforts of Desmond Tutu and Nelson Mandela to bring down apartheid, such a choice made a difference. The decision of amnesty and forgiveness in the land of the South Africa Truth and Reconciliation Commission has opened the way for greater faithfulness to the higher dimensions of the human spirit.

In an earlier chapter of Hebrews, one finds these words: "If ... every transgression or disobedience received a just penalty, how can we escape if we neglect so great a salvation?" (See Hebrews 2:2-3.) South African wise folk realized that no human being is exempt from transgression and disobedience. They understood the transcendence of pardon.

45

Pardon engenders forgiveness. Forgiveness is the choice to use tools of love rather than weapons of body or spirit. Forgiveness takes the wallop out of retaliation. It removes the sport from sinning. Forgiveness has the capacity to turn everything around toward faithfulness. Forgiveness frees us for a positive, productive way of living.

Nothing teaches about the faithfulness of another on a day-to-day measure as well as the devotion of a dog guide. Without an assist dog's faithfulness, obedience would be hollow and the dog guide's work would be faulty as well as sporadic. The building of trust, the nurture of faithfulness, and the awakening of devotion hinge on the dog handler's choice to forgive the little acts of recalcitrance along the way.

A necessary, quick leash correction may appear to remedy an immediate situation. However, it may not inspire the dog to avoid repeating the mistake. The addition a few paces later of affirming words, such as, "That's better," provides the nourishment that energizes trust.

When the dog guide's handler shows trust in the dog's capacity to do good work, that trust breeds confidence in the dog and generates a greater mutual trust. Small choices by a dog guide to be faithful to the work of leading brings greater faithfulness in return. The dog wants to do its best work. Devotion nurtures devotion.

Obedience gains a reason when it teams with a spirit of faithfulness. The full meaning of the covenantal part of obedience gains life within the heart of a dog guide. Leader Dog Dolley's readiness proved true. Her obedience came from a dog who as readily could have chosen to go her own way. However, she would work whenever summoned at any time of day or night.

A death call at 4 a.m. necessitating a six-block winter walk. The beckoning words, "Dolley, we need to ..." roused her from night sleep. Within the moment, she was awake and ready for action, making possible the presence of her pastor partner with the dying parishioner.

The intensity of these spontaneous, thinking aloud, "Dolley, we need to ..." words bypassed the usual dog handling commands. "Dolley, we need to ..." ignited the dog guide's diligence. The

46

woman could trust her obedience. The dog guide could trust that the woman would not ill-use this request for her own convenience.

Dogs trust solid ground. Animal instinct causes a dog to avoid walking over a metal grating with unknown space beneath it. In order to circumvent the slippery metal bars of a cattle guard on a western foot trail, Dolley located an alternate route and navigated the team through a narrow turnstile whose complexity would have baffled most other animals.

As a young working dog, Treasure hoped to avoid walking across a metal grate that approached the entrance of a Makah Indian museum. Locating no other route to the entry, he responded to the quiet intensity of Dee's, "We need to find the door." Rebuffing his self-protective response while listening to Dee's high praise at each step, he crossed the grating.

Several years later, as a result of his faithful work commitment, Treasure was able to guide his partner the three-block walk to the veterinarian when he was suffering with a bout of arthritis. He trusted her encouragement to go the slowed pace that he could manage. He remained faithful.

The woman's dog guides found early in their work lives that they could trust her to be fair. She would ask her assist dog to do something of extraordinary difficulty only when necessary. She would remain faithful to her side of the promise of teamwork. Trust breeds trust. Faithfulness brings faithfulness. Devotion generates devotion.

Paul was concerned about the Hebrews lest they begin to drift away from God and from their faithfulness. In today's scripture, he quoted the Hebrew prophet Jeremiah (31:33-34). He reminded the Hebrew folk about the promise that God made to "put [God's] laws on their hearts, and write them on their minds." Lifting up the next verse, Paul emphasizes, "[T]hen he adds, 'I will remember their sins and their misdeeds no more' " (v. 17).

Paul wrote to these early Christians about the ways of "provok[ing] one another to love and good deeds" (v. 24). He hoped they would practice tolerance and forgiveness as a high priority. Provoke seems an odd choice of word here, although it is a Pauline type of word.

Paul was good at urging church folk out of sluggishness. He could spur them into positive action with a verbal prod. He could rankle them out of passivity. He could incite them to persevere. Try that in today's congregations. Rather, think of provoking as challenging and stirring into action. To provoke is to go about something deliberately.

Apparently, as do modern Christians, the Hebrews practiced avoidance when apathy and discord threatened to take over. Paul told them that "not neglecting to meet together ... but encouraging one another" (v. 25) is the key to faithfulness. Forgiveness is personal. Forgiveness comes from within the heart. Forgiveness is also social, within relationship.

Paul reminds us that we must put the faithfulness of forgiveness into the action of kindling in others a similar faithfulness to the way of love and good deeds. Then obedience to societal rules and laws will become motivated by the heart. These guidelines then will be perceived as part of human concern.

Good Friday speaks of faithfulness that is wholehearted. Our faithfulness is not lip service, not on the surface. It is to be not on a Sunday only or on a Good Friday only faithfulness. It is to be the action of our whole being.

Our faithfulness has a model in Christ's action. In his living and his dying, his whole being focused upon "hope without wavering" (v. 23). Christ's capacity for forgiveness was a product of his faithfulness.

Nothing teaches us about the faithfulness of another on a day-to-day measure as well as the devotion of a dog guide, nothing that is, unless it is the faithful, obedient action of Christ on a cross on a Good Friday of long ago. "Let us hold fast to the confession of our hope without wavering, for he who has promised is faithful" (v. 23).

Easter
1 Corinthians 15:19-26

In Fact

On first reading of Paul's message to the Corinthians, two parts stand out: The first is a phrase, "In fact." Paul said, "But in fact Christ has been raised from the dead, the first fruits of those who have died" (v. 20). The second is his comment, "The last enemy to be destroyed is death" (v. 26).

First, "In fact." Fact is information presented as objectively real, a real occurrence, something having demonstrable existence. So says the American Heritage Talking Dictionary. Factual information has reality and actuality. Something authentic and certain grabs us about it. The idiom, in fact, means in reality or in truth.

In fact is a surprising choice of words to preface resurrection talk. In fact leaves little room for the every day doubt that invites us to wonder about life after death.

With similar characteristic directness, Paul also tells the Corinthian Christians, "The last enemy to be destroyed is death." Three days ago, our thoughts centered on Jesus' death. By natural progression, when we think of his death, we resume cogitation about our own death. Most of us, however, prefer to skip over Good Friday and jump straight to Easter.

Nevertheless, Easter thoughts lift us to the resurrection and then to our own life after death, that is, if *in fact* we allow ourselves to think about death at all. As the years and changes gain on us, we may try harder to keep pushing death back farther in the mind while, death *in fact* finds more opportunity to peck at our vulnerability.

The proximity of Good Friday to Easter reminds us that, unlike the first followers of Christ, we have the benefit of knowing on

Good Friday that Easter will come. Still, resurrection is a stumbling block for new pilgrims and for some continuing Christians.

We can stretch enough, maybe, to allow for one or two miracle stories. We, maybe, can even accept most of them, saying God has reasons for that sort of intervention. However, the miracle of the resurrection is different. We do not have that last piece to the puzzle. The jump seems too great for something deep within us to dare. Yet something equally deep within us yearns for resurrection to be *in fact*.

Let us approach death and resurrection in a more palatable fashion. I want to tell you about a family and a dog guide. We know the dog guide as the black Labrador/border collie named Leader Dog Treasure. The family, however, is an unusual gathering of men and women. With the exception of two folk who are age 58, they are between the ages of 80 and 97.

Picture a long, rather narrow room at the end of a hallway, like the crosspiece of a capital T. This room is known as the chapel to these care center residents. They also visit this space for small groups and exercise classes, but on Saturday mornings they come to play.

For an hour, five card tables are arranged in a line between the large windows at either end of the crosspiece. To these tables come about a dozen men and women. Most use wheelchairs. A couple use walkers. Occasionally someone enters on the arm of a caregiver.

Upon first glance, one might label these people as engaged in various stages of dying. If one listens for long, however, one notices that while their bodies or minds are in decline, all are also participants in resurrection.

They are readers of good poetry downloaded from web sites of libraries and universities and printed in type large enough for several to read. These folk are creators of poetry and stories. They engage in the creation of imaginative trips that take them far from the chapel room and return them refreshed in spirit. They speak always within the metaphor of living, dying, and new life but rarely address these themes directly.

Amid a myriad of "can no longer do" conditions, they have found the freedom of being who they are right now and doing what they can do on any given Saturday. Come meet these folk and discover how they became acquainted with resurrection.

Lorraine is keen minded, but the osteoporosis that has crumbled her spine keeps her in acute discomfort. Her curiosity to find out what the group will create with words each week temporarily uproots her pain and draws her to Saturday chapel.

Ernie, 58, lives with Huntington's disease. His listening is keen and, occasionally, he can utter a word distinct enough to be understood. As the result of a stroke, Lacy communicates only with her eyes.

With supplemental oxygen, a woman named Rowena finds enough energy for clarity of both speech and thought. She has found reasons to extend the capacity of her failing heart to its limit. She reads for the group. She relays to the nonvisual group leader the yes and no eye movements that are Lacy's responses to the facilitator's carefully worded questions. Lacy laughs aloud with the satisfaction of being understood. Rowena rejoices in understanding.

Rowena also interprets Ernie's garbled speech well enough to coax his continued trying. She colors her own contributions with a vivid imagination.

Their persistence rewards the tolerant patience of the rest of this family. Ernie has regained his sense of being a gentleman by remaining in the chapel until the leader has taken down all the card tables. With great concentration, he summons her dog guide, then hands the leader the dog's leash. His final responsibility is to turn off the lights.

Meet a few more of this family. The speech of Marian, who lives with multiple sclerosis, has become increasingly slower throughout the five years she has participated in the Saturday morning group. Sometimes her head becomes too heavy as she reads a passage of the group's writing. Her forehead bangs against the card table. Everything pauses until she has up righted herself.

Four other participants reflect various stages of cognitive exhaustion. With the leader's attentiveness to their moments of clarity, they also enjoy contributing.

Homer, Olive, and Vera are too fragile of body to remain in their homes, but they revel in the stimulation and challenge of the Saturday morning group. Homer exercises his once-thought-gone sense of fun and his belly laugh. Olive and Vera enjoy reading and the sense of community. In their words, "We wouldn't miss a single time. Sometimes we are thoughtful and sometimes we are silly. We never know what she is going to do next."

This resurrection began with Leader Dog Treasure. Given the option of watching for squirrels, he chose instead to relate to the folk sitting around the card tables. Moving quietly beneath the row of tables, Treasure sensed who especially needed him on a particular morning.

His quiet presence comforted new residents in the grief of transition. His refusal to leave the side of one woman who was beside herself with grouchiness melted her mood into calm. His docile but insistent nose nudging aroused sounds of enjoyment from deep within those who could barely hold a thought.

His sauntering down the hall to greet and escort some participants into the chapel room assured them they still count. His loving and accepting snuggles reawakened a warmth of spirit that had gone to sleep.

The tender attention of this sensitive dog altered the flat-lined voices of those who were drowning in boredom. He prompted the transposition of tones of isolation to the colorful voices of those who feel lovable.

Treasure clearly accepted each person regardless of capacity to think or move. He drew all of them from a living death of only waiting to restorative Saturday morning anticipation.

As this little group of individuals began to thrive on acceptance, they began to perceive each other as partners and trusted friends. The group became acquainted with the freedom of knowing that all were acceptable as they were. They practiced the art of escaping themselves while returning more fully to themselves.

Each again had a reason to be. Regular attendance was important. Someone needed to be there to read the large type transcriptions of last week's tape recordings of their work. Reading aloud for as long as the eye energy held out was acceptable even if it were only for two lines.

No matter what form Good Friday took in their lives, something of the brokenness took a break for an hour. The last enemy to be destroyed was death.

This family, whose composition and capability change over time, began its play with words by creating a poem using words that rhyme with dog. As a result of their rebirth of interest and vigor, the group recently completed a 16-chapter children's book about (what else but) a metaphor of life, death, and resurrection. They wrote the biography of a snowman. Many times during its writing, their laughter and good humor seeped through the crack between the closed doors at the end of the hall and coursed into the rooms of other residents. It was the sound of resurrection, *in fact*.

Alpha Dog

Today we begin the first of six Sundays of revelation, that is, The Revelation to John.[1] Many shy away from this final book of the Bible, placing it toward the off-the-deep-end category. Others dismiss it as, at best, the allowed metaphorical expression, and, at worst, the outrageous fantasy of one person. That person probably was John, the exiled pastor of several Asian churches. Still others avoid the book because of fear that it will tap into personal horrors or trigger negative fantasies.

We forget that all talk of what happens after life on earth is, at best, a metaphor. We can only conjecture for we have not been to the "after here." If we are primarily people overcome by the dark, then thoughts about after our earthly life turn to a review of our fears. Those who choose the light first, tend to opt for hope. It is all there in the book of Revelation, from the most scary fear to buoyant hope. The "how" of Revelation is not so important. It is the spirit of this book that returns us to hope.

Right away, John sets the tone. He writes, "To him who loves us and freed us from our sins by his blood, and made us to be a kingdom, priests serving his God and Father, to him be glory and dominion forever and ever. Amen" (vv. 5-6). John could have said instead, "To him who is about to scare the wits out of us," and sent us running from the book of Revelation forever.

The letter format, one of two techniques used in Revelation, comes at the beginning and at the conclusion of the book. In between is pure drama. Apocalyptic literature was popular among

Jews and Christians at the beginning of the Christian era. We, how-ever, are not used to this imagery and drama that attempts to dis-close the future.

John was concerned about the churches to whom he wrote. They were situated in the western provinces of Asia Minor. Known today as Turkey, this general region was then a mass of chaos, hav-ing been conquered by the Romans. The people of these churches suffered for their faith. They needed encouragement. They needed to know that God had a purpose for them and that God was for and with them. He wanted his churches to know that God is in charge.

God has always been in charge, from the beginning. God is in charge right now in this present time. Furthermore, God intends to be in charge in the time yet to come. These are reassuring words for anyone in the midst of chaos. These words help whether the churches are in Ephesus and Pergamum of long ago or they are in New York City on a September morning in 2001. When everything feels out of control, the question sharpens, "Who is in charge here, anyway? Someone, hear me and help!"

The lectionary reading schedule for the next six Sundays re-veals six truths from Revelation. These truths are messages of hope. This is the first truth: God is the beginning and the end, God who was, who is, who is to come, the Almighty. Second, when the song of hope within us has quieted, God puts a new song into our hearts. Third, salvation belongs to God and is for all people.

The remaining truths come from the final two chapters of Rev-elation. God promises to be present with us making all things new. As the one who lights our way, God has a vision of healing. The sixth truth, the invitation to come, is open for anyone who wishes to receive the water of life as a gift. These readings present a healthy dose of hope.

In light of the first truth, alpha God, let us return to our dog guide team. In a class of 25 dog guides at Leader Dogs for the Blind, there is an alpha dog. Two weeks into their team training, the class went for a country-style jaunt along a walking trail. Both the dogs and their partners saw this as a true outing. Having felt confined by the rigors of town training, they found on the trail a smoothness of pace that is impossible with the constant starts and

56

stops that street curbs require. The country walk was a release, albeit a disciplined release.

While engaged in this country walk, the woman found again her natural walking gait. It had a rhythm unlike her robotic cadence that had echoed the precise, mechanical tap of her mobility cane against a concrete path. No longer "thing-ified," she felt carefree and graceful while being led by a dog guide. This new experience returned her to a sense of wholeness. She felt like an alpha female teamed with an alpha female dog guide.

They strode together, tethered by a harness handle. Her hand felt every move of Dolley's muscles, every hesitation, and every intention. It must have been reciprocal as the dog with high wagging tail and right ear flopping caught her partner's sense of joy.

Leader Dog Dolley was the smallest of her classmates. Nevertheless, the 46-pound dog communicated clearly that she wanted to be in the lead — not only of her partner but of all the dog guide teams they passed along the walkway, even the 90-pound Shepherd.

For the moment, she was alpha dog in spirit, moving her partner in front of first one team and then another. She would lead the pack along the concrete trail while carefully attending to the person holding her harness. They were partners. They were also reprimanded after their grand airing because they had exceeded a safe working speed. Nevertheless, it was a joy walk and did wonders for the understanding and empathy of each other's true spirit. They would maintain this exuberant work spirit throughout the life of the team.

Until Dolley began to slow in her senior years of work life, they had moments of contention for who would be alpha within their team. Unlike any other assist dog, a dog guide must have enough of the alpha spirit to lead out and to guide so as to compensate for its partner's lack of sight. However, the dog guide also needs the capacity to consent to a human command. This is a delicate balance.

Revelation 1:8, the first of the six lectionary passages from this book, reads, " 'I am the Alpha and the Omega,' says the Lord God, who is and who was and who is to come, the Almighty." In the Bible, Alpha and Omega, used together, are found only three times.

The two other passages also come from the assigned pericopes of Revelation in the final two chapters: From 21:6, "I am the Alpha and the Omega, the beginning and the end." From 22:13, "I am the Alpha and the Omega, *the first and the last*, the beginning and the end."

From the beginning to the end of the Bible, God says to us, "I am." God started the "I am" with Moses when Moses was afraid to go do the work God had assigned him. "God said to Moses, 'I am who I am.' Further, he told Moses, 'Thus you shall say to the Israelites, "I am has sent me to you" ' " (Exodus 3:14). God said, "This is my name forever, and this is my title for all generations" (from Exodus 3:15).

Hear again the "I am." This time Jesus spoke them when he sent the disciples out into the world: "And remember," Jesus said, "I am with you always, to the end of the age" (Matthews 28:20).

Hear, also, John's telling later in the first chapter of Revelation about his vision of God in another form, one "like the Son of Man" who, seeing John's fright, said, "Do not be afraid; I am the first and the last. I was dead, and see, I am alive forever and ever" (from 1:13-18).

Alpha is a familiar term, alpha — the first, the most important, alpha female, alpha male, alpha dog, alpha God. Alpha, A, is the first letter of the Greek alphabet. Omega, Ω, is the twenty-fourth letter, the last letter.

John's story in Revelation is the story of a faithful, creating, and re-creating "God who is and was and who is to come." God as Alpha and Omega is present at the start and at the finish. Let us not worry about the time line or the form of God. Only trust this about God when you meet the difficult times in your life: God is. God is at all beginnings. God is at all endings. God is everywhere in between. This is the truth of God who is Alpha and Omega.

Is it not a similar sensing of God's Alpha and Omega in our lives that returns buoyancy to our spirits? From the beginning to the ending of you and me, God is saying deep into our souls, "I am."

1. I am indebted to a study of the book of Revelation led by Professor Gordon Brubacher, then at Doane College in Crete, Nebraska, given at the Nebraska Conference United Church of Christ Clergy Retreat in Grand Island, September 16-17, 1994.

Dog Song

What is it about the inner song that sings us? Is it a connecting with the singing of angels? Songs come from out of somewhere. Slave songs gave rhythm to the extended day of crop workers, girding them as they moved through long hours. Songs keep alive the souls of sweatshop workers in our day. You and I sing while engaged in tedious activity.

Some persons poke the radio button upon awakening in the morning and leave on the sound until nightfall. The sound could be anything — talk, music, whatever — to fill the space of silence and let us avoid listening to our thoughts. Just let the rhythm draw us into its charm.

You may yearn for a particular song. The ritual of your selection may necessitate a CD collection. The music we choose answers an inner calling. It accompanies the project undertaken. It counters the moment's mood. Such music becomes acceptable, tolerable sound that distracts us from the extraneous or from the unthinkable so we can concentrate.

What are the songs that have sung you through significant stages of your life? Was it a Mozart's "Alleluia" when you found your life mate or an "Agnus Dei" during a tragedy? Was it "For Unto Us A Child Is Given" for the adopted baby? Did it come as Brahm's "Lullaby" at another birth? Was it finding yourself a-hum when grandchildren came for a visit?

Inner songs sing us without prompting. Hymns come to mind when we need comfort and encouragement: "Be Still My Soul,"

61

"On Eagle's Wings," "There's A Bulb In Every Flower," "Joyful, Joyful, We Adore You." Every cell within vibrates with song.

One month after Dee's first dog guide, Dolley, came, a bittersweet song emerged from deep within. The dog became ill, the stress response of an immature dog guide who took her work more seriously than her puppy nature could manage.

Knowing the dog might not make it as a guide, Dee gentled and encouraged her. Between the necessary work commands of travel, she sang to Dolley. "Du, Du, Liebst Mir Im Hertzen" ("You, you, whom I love in my heart") sang itself as their song. "It spoke soul to soul," the woman said, "much as a parent lullabies a fretful baby."

The love song that had come from somewhere sang itself, crooning through woman to dog. The young dog took courage from Dee's tone of voice. Its warmth helped to strengthen Dolley's acceptability to herself. It coaxed her to carry out what became a long working partnership.

Neither the title nor the type of song that sings us matters. Song is the art form of the soul. Song is symbol. Song, even worded song, expresses the "beyond words" level of our being. Song shortcuts the communion connection with another time and another place.

Sometimes, no song comes. As the author of Revelation says, "[T]here was silence in heaven for about half an hour" (8:1). A half hour is long. Long, silent songless stretches, when we are struggling to hold on to life, seem to stop all movement of time. Is this difficult time also the time the angel begins to sing and to infuse us with new hope?

Do you believe in angel songs? Angels are as intangible as the sound of an idea entering the mind. They are as palpable as the sense of God's presence.

If angelic symbols of God's interest in our lives were the products only of the book of Revelation, we might be concerned. However, these messengers of God, these imparters of instruction, these doers of deeds, and these singers of song span both testaments of the Bible.

There are more than 225 references to angels, from the Genesis angel who found Hagar to the angel Gabriel who came first to Zechariah then visited Mary. The Gethsemane angel brought Jesus strength. An angel reassured the women at the Tomb.

For the ancients, angels spoke through music. Angels sang praises in the Psalms. A whole, heavenly host of angels sang the announcement of the birth of Jesus.

Must the angels sing to ensure and to assure that our spirit will survive? Our generic troubles, while wearing a unique face on each person, also existed in an earlier day. Reread Psalm 33, 40, 98, or 144. When life events squelch our inner song, these Psalms remind us that God "puts [a] new song into the mouths" of the angels. They announce another birth. This birth is within us this time. It is the rebirth of hope.

The song the angels sing in Revelation is no whispered song. We will not miss it. John describes the grand angelic choir of Revelation as "myriads of myriads" and "thousands of thousands" of angels gathered to sing "with full voice" (vv. 11-12).

This choir stirs "every creature in heaven and on earth and under the earth and in the sea, and all that is in them" to sing the song of "blessing and honor and glory and might" (v. 13). Stand back. This music rivals Handel's "Hallelujah Chorus."

Is the angels' song mania? Is it a button that John pokes, the in-language of his day? John's emphasis in Revelation on the angels' song is his way of summoning the seven churches of Asia. It is his way of calling us back to the birth, to the holy night of rejoicing throughout the heavens, to the star, to Christ. Is this choir of angels not also God's calling us back to hope through Christ after we have come through the Lenten days of turmoil and through the Good Friday of national emergencies? It calls us toward the Easter of our own life.

Each age sings its innate and unique expression of rich emotion. Listen to a contented child sing at play. Each era delivers its own song. The angels' songs in Revelation may have been the healing jazz of John's day. Who can read the contagious songs of joy in today's passage without an inner stirring of song? How fully John grasped that music is a response of the whole being. He knew well, also, the silence that precedes a new song.

The Revelation song stretches back to the Exodus Song of Moses: "I will sing to the Lord, for he has triumphed gloriously ... the Lord is my strength and my might, and he has become my salvation; this is my God, and I will praise him" (15:1-2).

John also knew Psalm 33. In fact, one might rename the book of Revelation, "John's Fantasy on the Theme of Psalm 33." Reread Psalm 33 in light of today's Revelation passage. Hear its promises that all waiting people, those from the seven churches of Asia and we, have hoped for all these years.

We can hear in Revelation other Psalms, also songs of both lament and praise. Hear Psalm 40:2-3: "He drew me up from the pit, out of the miry bog, and set my feet upon a rock, making my steps secure. He put a new song in my mouth, a song of praise to our God." From Psalm 96:6: "Honor and majesty are before him; strength and beauty are in his sanctuary." And from Psalm 144:9: "I will sing a new song to you, O God."

The Revelation song is a love song sung to Christ. This Song of the Lamb affirms and empowers. Its first word, "Worthy," is as reaffirming as the blessing, "My Son, my Chosen," the words on the brink of Jesus' first going forward with hope and blessing at his transfiguration. Jesus was alone at the transfiguration. Here, the whole crowd of angels affirms him. All bless him as not just generally worthy but worthy of it all, "power and wealth and wisdom and might" (vv. 12, 13).

Reminiscent of Job, the Revelation song sings, all of your effort, Jesus, your suffering, your life, was worth it. Your suffering and your faithfulness too, you people of the seven Asian churches, and ours too, sing this song.

Our inner song has a reason for us to discover. Our inner song draws us closer to God, bringing us strength as certain as that the angel's brought Jesus at Gethsemane. The words of our inner song may differ from the Song of Moses and the Song of the Lamb, but they return us to our own center. Our inner song reminds us of a still powerful, still worthy, still triumphing, and still present God, who still elicits from us in this new millennium a sense of awesome response, worship, and hope.

When we leave behind the classroom, the office work, the day job, the long professional hours, or the day's stress of whatever to spend time for ourselves, and get some rest, what happens? The "Song of You" slips in. Just like that, it hums. It whistles. It outright sings. Listen this week as your song begins to sing you.

Planted Paws

Leader Dog Treasure, Dee's second dog guide, developed a unique method of winter guiding when the team could not avoid icy conditions. The first icy night they worked together, they lasted only a few yards beyond the driveway of their home. Dee had slipped, startling Treasure. Then Treasure slid. This undermined his confidence. In wisdom, they turned back.

The next morning they returned to the same spot. This time the dog guide had a plan. He planted each paw as he walked. He snugged slightly against Dee's left knee as if to say, "I'm right here. Lean on me for stability. I will guide you through this icy mess."

In the worst of Nebraska's midwinter, the team abandoned their usual morning walking route that sprawls through the roads of the rural town. Instead, they covered the same distance by outlining an equal-sided inner cross of sidewalk borders formed by the blocks approaching the downtown intersection.

Late one winter, nature dropped a sheet of glaze ice along the north sidewalk of shops that lined the main street. None of Treasure's usual planting of the paw worked. No leaning slightly against the leg was of assistance. They could gain no footing. Again, their decision was consensual: Let's turn around and get out of here.

The following morning, having been forewarned that the swath of glaze also extended in front of the local hardware store, they remained on the sheltered side of the street until they reached the crossing in front of the store. Dee did not tell Treasure about the icy sidewalk but gave instead the directive to cross the street. By that time, the sidewalk might have been sanded. Nothing doing. Treasure exercised what the training school calls "intelligent disobedience."

The dog guide had made a visual check. He would not approach the sidewalk. Instead, he paralleled it. He led her behind a row of diagonally parked cars. Each time they came to a break between cars, the woman gave the "Find the sidewalk" command. Each time the dog guide planted his four paws. He refused to step onto the sidewalk until he finally spotted bare concrete.

Only some assist dogs have the capacity to become shepherds for persons who cannot see. A shepherd guides by definition. Its charge is to keep safe. It will not knowingly lead its partner into trouble.

Because a nonvisual person cannot make a visual safety judgment, the dog guide must. A guide for nonvisual persons must have the inner strength to refuse a command. It must also possess the grit strength to lead out when it ascertains the way is safe.

The action of intelligent disobedience surprises. It catches the attention. Even should the reason be a mystery or the action make little sense at first, to honor such a decision is integral to working within a relationship of trust. Only if both members of the dog guide team accept the dog's guide's freedom to refuse a command can such a partnership work.

As with any partnership, a team attitude invites the mutual respect of another's choices as well as the letting go of single-minded autonomy. This is not so different from a fruitful ecumenical partnership, a congregation, a marriage, parenting, a high school band, or an office work team. A team is a group of participants who are on the same side.

Let us enter today's passage from Revelation by asking what it tells us about God and about shepherding. As we stand watching with John and the elders on the sidelines, we see "a multitude of people" standing before the throne of Christ. This scene of the Revelation drama presents an intriguing picture because of its numbers and its composition.

The first lesson God imparts to us is that God is inclusive. More than a few people, John said, this was "a multitude of people robed in white." They came "from every nation, from all tribes and peoples and languages" (see v. 9).

Let us ponder these words in light of an inclusive multitude of people whose collective meaning speaks of unity. They reflect an openness about all people without restriction of physical ability, economic status, sexual or national orientation, or mind set.

Imagine the opportunity that ingathering must have been for the people of that diverse multitude. They would have learned to become inclusive themselves. They would have listened to and learned from each other along the way.

This is the second teaching from God: For God our active readiness is an indispensable component of our salvation. As with John's multitude, as we come through and out of great personal ordeals, we may also be so changed that others do not recognize us. We hardly know ourselves. "Who are these [people]?" the elder asked. John told the elder he should have recognized them, but they had changed.

We in turn ask what promotes such change. Growth is not a passive being done to but involves active participation. Sitting still and letting things happen to us brings little productive result.

Upon first reading, it seems a small point, but John did not report that the white robes these people were wearing had been washed by someone else. He said these people washed their own robes. They actively participated in cleaning up their own act. God wants us, also, to be proactive in our salvation.

Change, growth, and headway come from a similar listening to each other whether as a dog guide team, a multitude of pilgrims, or the shepherding of the Lamb of God. Like high school graduates after their first year of college, our readiness to grow also lets us absorb with passion what is offered us. We digest it and integrate it into a new being. We are changed. We are made whole by bringing all the parts of our being together in a unity.

What a rich, surprising mix of contrasting images we find in the book of Revelation. Among them are a throne and shepherd's field, clothes washed white from the red blood of a Lamb, shelter from one we might expect to punish, and talk of both desperation and hope.

Even this early however, in the seventh chapter of this revealing 21-chapter drama, the story is of hope. When we too are ready, when we too have washed our own metaphorical robes, we too will find ourselves transported to another spiritual place, the place of security and salvation.

The holy shelter God provides at the metaphorical spring of the water of life is simply that, shelter, not punishment. For those who make the journey, God provides salvation.

When we come to the book of Revelation, we revisit this journey of being saved from ourselves and for ourselves. We hear again that the good news of the Easter story is God's saving us from the harrowing and confining dimensions of ourselves. God saves us for the stretch and expansion of our fullest selves. God saves us for the unity of enriching the wider community.

Surprised? This is the third teaching of God: God recognizes that we need a shepherd to guide us toward what will bring us life. Listen to the language. Twenty-three times in this book, John refers to Christ as the Lamb. Christ is neither a reluctant nor a recalcitrant lamb but a triumphant, elevated Lamb seated in a high place.

The imagery is rustic. John's people knew about shepherds, lambs, gentleness, and the need for guidance. Not only are we like lambs with a shepherd, but Christ, our shepherd, also has the guidance of a shepherd. Jesus is the Lamb of God.

You and I do not always move willingly toward the springs that hold the water of life. Distraction dulls our homing sense. Even when the yearning is there, we seem unable to find these springs by ourselves.

We need someone to point the direction. Sometimes that shepherd is a dog guide whose actions show, "I will guide you through this mess." Sometimes it is another person who walks a few paces with us. Sometimes it is an ideal that draws us forward.

When we have chosen the right one to shepherd us toward the vitality of the human spirit and when we have come through change, like the cleansing that makes dirty clothes bright, we are ready to find the spring. There we find not God to fear, but God who says, "I'm right here to guide you."

Finally, let us return to the first words from this multitude, "Salvation belongs to our God." Surprised? This is God's fourth teaching: God's goal is to save us. The God who meets us is a savior so gentle and knowing of us that this savior is ready and waiting to "wipe away every tear."

Vocabulary Building

Just like that, everything changes. Another season of growing and schooling is just about over for the year. Nowhere do the chapters change so quickly as in the raising of a family. Every new learning is a first thing — first word, first step, first day of school, first everything.

First things pass away before our eyes. We can trust that to happen. We can trust that new things will come into being at every age. At all stages of life, some things are gone. Then the new bursts in and we strengthen our vocabulary of hope.

In the world of a dog guide, too, just as all seems to be going smoothly, the new has a way of slipping in. Dog guiding teaches the fine art of possibility, patience, and hope.

While walking at a pace commensurate with its partner's needs, a dog guide also is trained to exert a modicum of pull on its harness. This tension enables the assist dog to guide its partner around obstacles they encounter as well as to keep their course straight.

Late in Leader Dog Dolley's work life, it became necessary to make a change from working from the left side of Dee to working from the right. Upon consultation with school training staff, Dee gained assurance that even an older dog guide could adapt. In fact, the trainer said, the dog had been adjusting successfully to subtle changes in her partner for the last nine years. This transition, however, would require the dog to learn a new vocabulary for right-sided guiding.

They were to proceed slowly and with care so as not to overwhelm the dog. The adjustment worked. Eventually, she became adept at alternating the working side as needed. It was possible to move beyond the calamity of change to find the new possibility that change brings.

Dee's next dog guide would be trained using an adaptive, no-pull technique that would communicate by the dog's steadiness of pace and its proximity to its partner. Five years into the career of this second guide, additional physical changes called for the woman to find a way of holding the harness without grasping it with her hand.

Again she consulted the school. Again called upon to accommodate, she retrained this dog guide to work with a tool shaped like a shepherd's hook. She slipped her working hand into a hand splint to which had been affixed a stainless steel bar that would clutch the harness handle.

It was tricky. Were one of the team out of position, the tension would release and the shepherd's hook would slip off the handle. Leader Dog Treasure exercised an extra measure of patience. The sensitive dog had to accept first that he had done nothing wrong when the handle slipped. Then, he learned to pause mid-step whenever the hook slipped and wait for his partner to re-attach it. The adaptation worked.

Change works. God finds a way to introduce the new. God is in the business of making all things new. While God is busy re-creating possibility, you and I are busy consciously or unconsciously figuring out how we are going to meet the changes that interrupt our ease.

These changes call for finding a can-do attitude similar to that offered by Leader Dog staff. They require a letting go of what no longer works. They invite treasuring that other attachment when love turns to cherish and duty to devotion.

Even without the extraordinary adaptations a dog guide may be asked to make in its career, the bond it shares with its human partner cements early. After her first dog guide retired, the woman promised she would not let herself become as close to her next dog guide. She thought she had held back then noticed that love had turned again to cherish.

74

When does love become cherish? How do we keep from getting so attached?

An acquaintance whose family was moved around at the caprice of the spouse's employer had long since ceased to develop friendships of any depth. She said leaving was too painful and too frequent to grow a friendship.

Her neighbor, on the other hand, was the daughter of a career service person. She had learned early on to make good friends and to cherish them for as long as possible. Of course, she said, losing those friends was disquieting, but living within the impoverishment of a friendless person would have been more costly.

Perhaps rather than asking the impossible, that is, how we can keep from becoming so attached in the first place, other queries would be more fruitful. How do we make the right kind of attachments with those who are special to us? How do we relate to the evanescent dimensions of our lives? How do we handle the temporary? How do we wade through all the mud of disruption, leap over all the uncertainty, and trust God as true?

"[And God] said, 'See, I am making all things new.' Also he said, 'Write this, for these words are trustworthy and true' " (v. 5).

Something breaks down — an arm or a hand, a plan or a spirit. Our path goes askew. Disquiet smudges internal rhythm until it jerks out of sync. Then some inner thrust impels us forward again.

Change is possible. Change works. Without taking the mystery out of change, a sign of God's presence lessens our fear of it. God keeps introducing new people into our lives.

When it is right, the mystery of a new relationship answers itself. When it is right, a new idea presents itself. When it is right, a new capacity and a new way of proceeding come into being.

We change. We true up our essential selves. We become a new creation.

In these lines from his song poem, "Moonless,"[1] C. "Howie" Howard, a young poet, composer, and "folkrok" musician studying at Doane College in Crete, Nebraska, snatches a piece of the energy of this new creation:

I'm so glad I found this beat again
The music dances to my soul
You raise your hands and stamp your feet again and
Make me whole.

God is always making all things new: new creation, the capacity to heal in body and spirit, the renewal we gain after a time of re-creation, the expectant sense of nothing in history being finished but always campaigning for improvement, a natural world that practices re-creating itself each spring. Some things are gone and then there is the new.

God is continually creating. God is not a stagnant God. Neither is God satisfied with the old or the status quo when it needs to change. In the book of Revelation, the word "new" appears six times: "A new name" (2:17), "a new Jerusalem" (3:12, 21:2), "a new song" (5:9, 13:3), "a new heaven" (v. 1), "a new earth" (v. 1), and "I am making all things new" (v. 5). If you are counting, "life" wins in Revelation. The word appears twenty times.

All the little bits and pieces of change point to the final change. We call it final, yet perhaps it is only another change. Think about an Uncle Buford, recently diagnosed with bone cancer and consider the time line for what lies ahead. Think about a woman named Serena, in her third year of surviving bone cancer and able to focus again on something other than her discomfort, even forgetting, almost, that she lives with a chronic disease.

Think about another friend, Ronald, who was making a delivery and found himself off the highway with a shovel during a snowstorm and only seconds to reflect before his heart gave out and he was gone at age 64. Think about Bruce, whose brain disorder makes it impossible for him to concentrate long-term at anything.

Somehow, it takes most of us a lifetime to become comfortable with the reality that our being here will change. We may die from a cancer or a coronary, or we might live through it. However it plays out, the important thing is to find time to cherish what is for us to cherish, to look with our eyes, to hear and listen, to savor moments of intimacy, and to waste as little time as possible on letting go of what no longer works.

This cherishing does not need clock time. Learning to cherish enables us to put time into its proper perspective and become fascinated with a new, strangely timeless journey. As we grieve for the losses that change brings our way, may we also find peace within what we find.

"See, the home of God is among mortals. [God] will dwell with them; they will be [God's] peoples, and God himself will be with them; [God] will wipe every tear from their eyes" (vv. 3-4). Just like that, everything is made new.

---

1. Shared by permission. Copyright Christopher L. Howard, 2001.

Easter 6
Revelation 21:10, 22—22:5

Red Light, Green Light

Only in a farming community would it happen ... Leader Dog Dolley and her partner had crossed the street at the corner of First National Bank and the Coast-To-Coast Store in West Point, Nebraska. Half a block later, the dog guide stopped short upon hearing someone huffing behind them.

It was the fellow from the hardware store. He was not sure she should trust her dog, he said. He had been looking out the window, he said, and wanted to be sure the woman knew her guide had disobeyed. The dog had crossed the street on a red light, he said.

With the absence of color recognition and the unavailability in most towns of bird chirping, that is, vocal walk signals, neither a dog guide nor its partner can know which light click means red and which indicates green. Instead, both the guide and the handler attend to other clues such as the movement of traffic parallel to their intended route, the absence of traffic sounds, or the pedestrian flow.

When approaching a crossing, a nonvisual person has little way of knowing how far the cycle of a traffic light has proceeded. The team must wait until the click sounds that indicates a signal change. At times, that brings a considerable wait.

The shopkeeper probably nodded his head in puzzlement when Dee explained that such a crossing is allowed by mutual consent. After waiting through one complete cycle of signal changes, if the team discerns that no traffic is coming, they cross the street.

The shopkeeper had been watching them work together, not attending to traffic conditions. He also had been too far away to have heard the second click of the signal box.

So finely tuned was the connection between this particular dog guide and its partner that, without full knowledge or precise understanding, they had in the same breath each started to move forward, proceeding together across the street.

The book of Revelation, also, is about making connections without complete understanding. Today's reading is the part of chapters 21 and 22 that draw together three symbolic strongholds long familiar to the people of John's time. These strongholds are the metaphors of light, the image of the river of the water of life, and the tree of life. They permeate scripture and point to hope.

Always, our God has been and is an interactive God. Always there is a two-way responsibility, the bond of keeping promises by both God and the human family. Always, the rainbow connection shows itself.

John beckons us in Revelation to recognize our human condition and to find in our lives the light and presence of God. He speaks of God as the new light and the lamp, a light so strong that "nations will walk by its light" and the rulers of "the earth will bring their glory into it" (v. 24). He reminds us of this heritage of light.

From the great light in the night that led the shepherds and wise folk to the manger to the great light of sunrise of Easter morning, we remember this light. Returning us to the Hebrew Scriptures, John draws us to the words of the writer of Isaiah with his theme of God's promise of purpose, "I am the Lord, I have called you in righteousness. I have taken you by the hand and kept you; I have given you as a covenant to the people, a light to the nations" (Isaiah 42:6).

John invites our ears to hear again the Psalmist sing of the hope that God's presence brings into the bleak times of our lives, "Even the darkness is not dark to you; the night is as bright as day, for darkness is as light to you" (Psalm 139:12).

John calls us back to the beginning when "God said, 'Let there be light'; and there was light. And God saw that the light was good" (Genesis 1:3-4). We recognize the light that comes into the sky as a rainbow of God's promise. It is an offering to us of a covenantal relationship. Our task is to make the connection between God's light and our light.

Always, the goal of our God has been and is the healing of nations and the healing of persons. In another connecting, the vision of hope must have been heartening to the first Christians. At the end of the first century, they were undergoing a second round of persecution by the Romans. Such constant struggle can bring death to the human spirit.

"[T]he river of the water of life," a full, crystal clear stream flanked on either side with "the tree of life" would have provided enough variety of fruit to get them through an entire year of changing seasons. It would sustain the spirit and their being in a difficult time. (See vv. 1-2.) Their story would be one of survival.

The book of Revelation stands in close connection with the Hebrew Scriptures. A large number of verses in Revelation comes from these earlier scriptures. The imagery of the river of the water of life and the tree of life is a direct replay of the vision of the Hebrew prophet Ezekiel. (See Ezekiel 47:12.) In the book of Ezekiel, another example of apocalyptic literature, God told Ezekiel about the equal division of the land for the inheritance of the twelve tribes of Israel. The source of this river was also a temple, the temple to be rebuilt after another season of persecution and desolation.

"See now," God also told these struggling, exiled people of Israel to whom disaster upon disaster came, "I am for you," (Ezekiel 36:9). Do the people of today's Israel reread the hardships and the promises of their heritage as we reread the hardships and promises told in Revelation? Do they also find a God who says, still, " 'I am for you,' and I will help you rebuild your lives"?

God has always entered and will always enter the turmoil and the mess. God nurtures, nourishes, and heals. God meets death with life. God counters starvation with the provision of health-giving food. God quenches thirst with good water, crystal clear.

What is more, the angel who showed John the river of the water of life and the tree of life invited him to look also at the leaves on that tree. The leaves "are for the healing of the nations" (v. 2).

This is a story of hope. It is the story of creation wanting to continue. God is a creating God. Again with this God who continually makes connections, there is a role of responsibility by the people. It is not just all given to the people. We will contribute. We have the charge to connect and to bring into this light "the glory and the honor of the nations" (Revelation 22:26).

Have you ever tuned to the Saturday afternoon opera on public radio after the musical story has already begun? You might not recognize the language, although some of the themes sound familiar to you. You have the choice of turning off the radio or sitting back to listen to the music with your heart. Should you choose the latter, you might find that you are imbibing the spirit of the opera. You might come to understand the story through its music at a level that needs no translation of word or explanation of libretto.

Similarly, a visit with the book of Revelation is not so much an attempt to unravel a puzzle of images and unusual happenings. It is more like choosing to sit back and listen with the heart, to acknowledge the scary parts without needing to understand them because we already know what it is like to be afraid. We already know the yearning of the human family because we are part of that fragile yet enduring family. We already have the capacity to feel the strength and trust of a faithful God because we have been given to recognize hope.

Ascension Of The Lord
Ephesians 1:15-23

Holy Collision

Before a dog guide and its teammate meet, an apprentice pup spends twelve months in the home of a 4-H family. Under their tutelage it learns the basic socialization of such behaviors as not lifting the steak off a restaurant patron's plate as the dog walks past a booth.

After that first year, the dog enters the next sequence of training where it works at the training facility with five trainers. Trainer/dog teams concentrate on command vocabulary, walking pace, and a curriculum of other skills essential to dog guiding. For the final month of that eight month period the future human partner trains with the dog guide at the school.

When Dee began training, the training captain told the students in the first lecture, "Despite all this instruction and even though your guide dog had a session with a trainer wearing a blindfold, it does not really understand yet about blindness. One day, however, something will happen," she said. "It will know unequivocally what its purpose is in life."

Sure enough, on day five, Leader Dog Dolley found the vocation she was to follow with keen devotion. Their dorm room was at the far end of the hall from the student phone. As Dolley lay tethered in her sleep alcove. Dee sprawled on the bed. The loud speaker reported, "Dee, your husband's on the phone."

Dee forgot the guide dog who was to accompany her everywhere. She forgot even where she was, and forgot, also, to allow for the wall that abutted the recessed area. She took off in a sprint and ran head on into the protruding wall.

Dolley witnessed this collision. Suddenly for the dog, Dee was no longer just a friendly companion. Her "person" could not see where she was going. The dog knew it must guide her. With that revelation, Dolley was no longer just a dog. With the eyes of her heart enlightened, she had become a Leader Dog. Transformed, she was serious with purpose and mission now. With this mutual empowerment, the dog guide and the woman moved forward as a team.

Revelation sometimes comes to us as a slow series of passages, a lifetime of telling itself with little bits and pieces of hope to keep us going. Revelation also can come with as abrupt a dawning as banging into a wall. The book of Revelation is a holy collision of reality with reality, that is, the reality of struggle with the reality of hope.

The first century after Jesus' life was a time of heavy persecution. The people of that day also needed a vision of hope. They needed release to a better situation. Paul countered their attacks of hopelessness with a vision and dream of hope.

He prayed these words for the church at Ephesus: "I pray that the God of our Lord Jesus Christ, the Father of glory, may give you a spirit of wisdom and revelation as you come to know [God], so that, with the eyes of your heart enlightened, you may know what is the hope to which [God] has called you" (vv. 17-18).

This segment of the lectionary readings for today leaves the book of Revelation. It returns us to Paul's words. The Ephesians passage completes the sequence that we began with Paul's words on Ash Wednesday.

These two verses from the letter to the Ephesians unite the pre-Easter Pauline passages with those post-Easter Revelation selections that have drawn us toward the ascension of Christ. Today, forty days after Easter, is Ascension Sunday. Today we celebrate rising to a new level of spiritual being. Ascension Sunday begins the empowerment of a new community, that we call the church.

Paul is practical. In the words, "a spirit of wisdom and revelation," he reminds us to marry the wisdom of an intentional and clear mind with an openness for what might be revealed within our heart. Paul's prayer is for one united spirit of wisdom and revelation. He suggests that our relationship to God is similar to the journey of two who meet first as strangers. Then they come to know each other in a fullness of understanding.

In the book of Revelation, John's artistic expression of the collision between wisdom and revelation is as pure fantasy as the impressionist Van Gogh's painting, *Wheat Field Under Clouded Sky*, or a jazz improvisation of "Just A Closer Walk With Thee."

When jazz instrumentalists jam, they honor a basic tune. The group begins by playing together the straight melody of "Just A Closer Walk With Thee." One by one, each musician improvises on the theme. Each successive improvisation carries the strain nearly beyond recognition. It transports listeners toward a still-fuller understanding of the music. Borders blur between the performer, the instrument, and the listener, revealing the truth of the song and the truth of ourselves to ourselves.

First time attendees at a jam session in New Orleans soon learn that applause mid song is not rudeness. It is ready acknowledgment of each musician's successive revelation of the composer's intent. During *Jazz*, Ken Burns' PBS series about the history of jazz, Lloyd Schulz commented, "Don't wait until the song is finished." So it is, may we suggest, that we need not reserve our admiration for the end. Instead, we should rejoice in each successive piece of understanding of heart and mind that we gain.

Sometimes when revelation comes to us, it is a holy collision of one reality with another. Revelation bumps into us at Van Gogh's horizon line between a farmer's wheat field standing ripe for harvest and a bank of impending clouds hanging dark with hail.

The terror of revelation collides with the jubilance of revelation. With equal certainty, fast moving storm clouds can turn and blow to the north of a field, opening again the ready crop to the hope of drying sunshine and loaves of bread. With destruction aborted, creation again follows the design of its creator.

In the book of Revelation, the apprehension of looking at the reality of ourselves as God sees us collides with the grace of that same loving and forgiving creator. God wants continually to make us new. Like a gift of impressionistic art or a musical improvisation, the book of Revelation offers a pathway. This pathway can expand us beyond ourselves as it leads us to a fuller understanding of the inner person.

The dawning of responsibility, ours, for our actions, our decisions, attitudes, prejudgings, and dreams comes with equal candor. We recognize our choices toward meaningful living and toward the rising of a clearer sense of purpose. We attain as astute a perception of the driving power of hope as a dog guide that knows why it is a dog guide.

We become acquainted with God, with God's fullness of hope for us, and with the empowerment of the church through the risen Christ. This also may come as levels of gradual enlightenment. This unveiling resembles the hope of a composer. As a congregation of jazz musicians explores and expands the theme of a musical composition, the musicians perceive and convey the full expression of the composer.

With this fullness of spirit in wisdom and revelation, we come to know God. We become cognizant of the hope to which God has called us. We gain a sense of the riches of our inheritance as children of God and the greatness of God's empowerment in our lives and in the world. This strength does not just sit there but frees person, church, and world for wholeness.

Revelation "of the hope to which [God] has called us" (v. 17) can come as a dawning as sudden as a prairie sunrise with early, day-birthing sun that startles wind into unsettled gusts. Then, up, sun stands suspended — silent, full power surveying the possibility of a new day.

The Tantalizing "Come"

More than anything else, Edward wanted God to forgive Keith. More than anything else, he wanted to forgive his son for taking his own life. For several months after his son's suicide, Edward feared that Keith was lost. The father could speak to no one about his heartbrokenness.

Then, prompted by the open, sky-filled space as he drove with friends across the prairie of Nebraska, he turned to the couple in the rear seat and told them the following dream:

> *I noticed someone walking in the distance. The person wore my son's favorite red plaid flannel shirt. I looked more closely. It was my son. I followed Keith at a safe but curious distance. Then I looked up. There stood another man. He also wore a red plaid flannel shirt. The second man stood facing my son, and I recognized him. It was Christ. Jesus' open and welcoming arms were beckoning Keith to come to him.*

The faithful Christian said he did not know if his dream were fantasy, wishful thinking, a sign of his own precarious state of mind, or what it was. All he knew for certain, he said, was that something had melted within him, some of the anger and some of the fear.

The dream was a gift. The image of his son enfolded in Christ's compassionate hug had begun to replace the picture of the closed casket. The dream comforted him. A piece of the grief had melted away to reveal a quiet reassurance. "Come, it is I, Jesus, waiting to welcome you." He knew from this curious distance that his son was now safe.

"Come ... It is I, Jesus." With arms opening and welcoming, the word is "Come," the little word, "Come."

A slather of molasses on concrete is one stratagem of obedience training at dog guide school. One morning, leashed dogs on the way to their assigned sections in the relief area encounter a big blob of molasses at one sidewalk intersection.

The idea is for the curious dog to ignore that tempting scent without so much as a sniff. Several dogs do pass by the lure. Most succumb to the call of the molasses, necessitating a swift leash correction. Were it laced with toxic matter, such yielding to this succulent bait out in the work world could mark the end of an assist dog's life.

Working within a covenant of shared responsibility is imperative for a dog guide and its user. Soon after the new team first comes home, another, equally seductive testing period begins. Now, in the absence of the commanding eye of a school instructor, the dog is tempted to reassert dominance. This is no time for the human partner to yield to the temptation to give the dog a relaxing off-leash run. Off leash, the dog might choose not to come.

It has to want to come before it will respond to the invitation of its blind partner. It must choose to ignore the tantalizing "Come" of someone calling its name from across the street, the stranger's whistling, and the friend enticing it with a morsel of food. It must concentrate on its work.

The little word, "Come," is a come-no-matter-what issue. When, for a dog guide, does "Come" move beyond a necessary request to the obedient answer of devotion?

When for us does the response become devotion? The vocal equivalent of opening and welcoming arms, the word is "Come."

"Come," not "Get over here, now," but "Come." Not, come so I can hurt you, but come so I can praise you. Come has to do with mutual respect, a head held high, a high-wagging tail, and a ready-for-whatever trust.

The voice of a dog handler moderates any sharp edge of threat. It avoids a coaxing tone that would invite teasing or demean the equity of the work relationship. The bonding, "Come," conveys a quiet, respectful authority.

This earnest yet insistent "Come" that promises the immediate reward of a verbal praise or a pat promotes the growth of mutual respect. To a dog guide, "Come" is an invitation to work. It says, "I respect the dog part of you that is easily distracted. I respect the guide part of you that thirsts to work." The dog senses that respect and the respect becomes shared.

With this attitude, "Come" becomes a tool of instant understanding. When Leader Dog Treasure allowed a barking dog to rattle her or a squirrel to distract, the command returned concentration to his work.

For Dolley, "Come" said, "Are you ready to work?" "Come" was a sweet word because she lived to work. In later years, she appreciated the steadying persistence of "Come" that aided her focus. How unlike that is the ill-treated dog that shies toward its handler with rump lowered and tail half between its legs, the tip end still wagging with the mixed anticipation of fear and wanting to please.

What is the sound of God's "Come" that disarms our reserve? The other words of come carry little weight in God's come. Hear them: Coax, urge, demand, entice, implore, insist, order, persuade. Sometimes "Come" presents no words at all but stands waiting as open and welcoming arms.

Like the first "Come" of Advent, the "Come" of Revelation is an offer. When we finally hear God's "Come" in our hearts, the invitation answers the yearning of our wanting and our needing to come. Our "Come" that calls out to God intersects with God's "Come" that calls to us.

"Come" requires the readiness to hear that "Come" is a welcoming word. It is a welcome. It is an inclusive invitation.

What are the prerequisites of our readiness?

Hear again what "Come" tells us in today's short segments from the closing chapter of Revelation. Each message is simple, "Come." Each successive verse tells us more about "Come."

First, from verses 12-14, "See, I am coming soon; my reward is with me, to repay according to everyone's work." He counsels us to pay attention, to do our part, and to "wash [our] robes" first so we will be ready. That is, we need to make our own preparations. Clean the dirt from our lives. Make ourselves presentable. Clean up the inner pollution of the soul.

The second segment, from verse 16, reads, "It is I, Jesus...." This "I am" returns us to the record in Exodus of God's telling a reluctant Moses, "I am who I am" (Exodus 3:14). "It is I, Jesus" reminds us to pay attention to who is bidding us to come. Christ, God, is the grounding root of the church. "It is I" returns us to the empowerment of our own, "I am."

In the third passage, from verse 17, the Spirit and the bride say, "Come." A bride, a woman who is about to be married or is newly married, makes preparations for her new life. Earlier, in the third of five references to "bride" (Revelation 21:2), John defined bride as the new Jerusalem. Let us view this come as a starting point, the readiness of a bride about to enter a new relationship. To come is to accept and to begin a covenantal relationship of mutual promises.

What an open, welcoming anticipation enters as John expands the meaning of come: "And let everyone who hears say, 'Come' " (v. 17). This universal invitation would welcome diversity of physical ability, professional and economic status, sexual orientation, and national heritage, as well as the sticking points of human relationship in the early days of the church.

John continues in verse 17, "And let everyone who is thirsty come." Welcome, come as well, whether we thirst to see, to hear, to walk unassisted, to think clearly, or whatever else causes us to yearn. Come as well, regardless of our addictions, our emotional upheavals, our illnesses of brain and body, and whatever else threatens to paralyze the human spirit. Everyone is welcome at this table of wholeness. This state of being is a welcoming place.

John packs still more invitation into verse 17: "Let anyone who wishes take the water of life as a gift." "Come" carries neither burden nor charge. It is gift.

Finally, verse 20 hopes, "Surely I am coming soon." Rather than a put off, a sometime, or a when, "soon" is a promise that invites patience. Ready, we respond to this promise with open and welcoming hearts, "Amen. Come, Lord Jesus!"

Lectionary Preaching After Pentecost

The following index will aid the user of this book in matching the correct Sunday with the appropriate text during Pentecost. All texts in this book are from the series for the Second Readings, Revised Common Lectionary. (Note that the ELCA division of Lutheranism is now following the Revised Common Lectionary.) The Lutheran designations indicate days comparable to Sundays on which Revised Common Lectionary Propers or Ordinary Time designations are used.

(Fixed dates do not pertain to Lutheran Lectionary)

Fixed Date Lectionaries *Revised Common (including ELCA) and Roman Catholic*	**Lutheran Lectionary** *Lutheran*
The Day of Pentecost	The Day of Pentecost
The Holy Trinity	The Holy Trinity
May 29-June 4 — Proper 4, Ordinary Time 9	Pentecost 2
June 5-11 — Proper 5, Ordinary Time 10	Pentecost 3
June 12-18 — Proper 6, Ordinary Time 11	Pentecost 4
June 19-25 — Proper 7, Ordinary Time 12	Pentecost 5
June 26-July 2 — Proper 8, Ordinary Time 13	Pentecost 6
July 3-9 — Proper 9, Ordinary Time 14	Pentecost 7
July 10-16 — Proper 10, Ordinary Time 15	Pentecost 8
July 17-23 — Proper 11, Ordinary Time 16	Pentecost 9
July 24-30 — Proper 12, Ordinary Time 17	Pentecost 10
July 31-Aug. 6 — Proper 13, Ordinary Time 18	Pentecost 11
Aug. 7-13 — Proper 14, Ordinary Time 19	Pentecost 12
Aug. 14-20 — Proper 15, Ordinary Time 20	Pentecost 13
Aug. 21-27 — Proper 16, Ordinary Time 21	Pentecost 14
Aug. 28-Sept. 3 — Proper 17, Ordinary Time 22	Pentecost 15
Sept. 4-10 — Proper 18, Ordinary Time 23	Pentecost 16
Sept. 11-17 — Proper 19, Ordinary Time 24	Pentecost 17
Sept. 18-24 — Proper 20, Ordinary Time 25	Pentecost 18

Sept. 25-Oct. 1 — Proper 21, Ordinary Time 26	Pentecost 19
Oct. 2-8 — Proper 22, Ordinary Time 27	Pentecost 20
Oct. 9-15 — Proper 23, Ordinary Time 28	Pentecost 21
Oct. 16-22 — Proper 24, Ordinary Time 29	Pentecost 22
Oct. 23-29 — Proper 25, Ordinary Time 30	Pentecost 23
Oct. 30-Nov. 5 — Proper 26, Ordinary Time 31	Pentecost 24
Nov. 6-12 — Proper 27, Ordinary Time 32	Pentecost 25
Nov. 13-19 — Proper 28, Ordinary Time 33	Pentecost 26
	Pentecost 27
Nov. 20-26 — Christ The King	Christ The King

Reformation Day (or last Sunday in October) is October 31 (Revised Common, Lutheran)

All Saints' Day (or first Sunday in November) is November 1 (Revised Common, Lutheran, Roman Catholic)

U.S. / Canadian Lectionary Comparison

The following index shows the correlation between the Sundays and special days of the church year as they are titled or labeled in the Revised Common Lectionary published by the Consultation On Common Texts and used in the United States (the reference used for this book) and the Sundays and special days of the church year as they are titled or labeled in the Revised Common Lectionary used in Canada.

Revised Common Lectionary	Canadian Revised Common Lectionary
Advent 1	Advent 1
Advent 2	Advent 2
Advent 3	Advent 3
Advent 4	Advent 4
Christmas Eve	Christmas Eve
Nativity Of The Lord / Christmas Day	The Nativity Of Our Lord
Christmas 1	Christmas 1
January 1 / Holy Name of Jesus	January 1 / The Name Of Jesus
Christmas 2	Christmas 2
Epiphany Of The Lord	The Epiphany Of Our Lord
Baptism Of The Lord / Epiphany 1	The Baptism Of Our Lord / Proper 1
Epiphany 2 / Ordinary Time 2	Epiphany 2 / Proper 2
Epiphany 3 / Ordinary Time 3	Epiphany 3 / Proper 3
Epiphany 4 / Ordinary Time 4	Epiphany 4 / Proper 4
Epiphany 5 / Ordinary Time 5	Epiphany 5 / Proper 5
Epiphany 6 / Ordinary Time 6	Epiphany 6 / Proper 6
Epiphany 7 / Ordinary Time 7	Epiphany 7 / Proper 7
Epiphany 8 / Ordinary Time 8	Epiphany 8 / Proper 8
Transfiguration Of The Lord / Last Sunday After Epiphany	The Transfiguration Of Our Lord / Last Sunday After Epiphany
Ash Wednesday	Ash Wednesday
Lent 1	Lent 1
Lent 2	Lent 2
Lent 3	Lent 3
Lent 4	Lent 4
Lent 5	Lent 5
Passion / Palm Sunday (Lent 6)	Passion / Palm Sunday
Holy / Maundy Thursday	Holy / Maundy Thursday
Good Friday	Good Friday
Resurrection Of The Lord / Easter	The Resurrection Of Our Lord

Easter 2	Easter 2
Easter 3	Easter 3
Easter 4	Easter 4
Easter 5	Easter 5
Easter 6	Easter 6
Ascension Of The Lord	The Ascension Of Our Lord
Easter 7	Easter 7
Day Of Pentecost	The Day Of Pentecost
Trinity Sunday	The Holy Trinity
Proper 4 / Pentecost 2 / O T 9*	Proper 9
Proper 5 / Pent 3 / O T 10	Proper 10
Proper 6 / Pent 4 / O T 11	Proper 11
Proper 7 / Pent 5 / O T 12	Proper 12
Proper 8 / Pent 6 / O T 13	Proper 13
Proper 9 / Pent 7 / O T 14	Proper 14
Proper 10 / Pent 8 / O T 15	Proper 15
Proper 11 / Pent 9 / O T 16	Proper 16
Proper 12 / Pent 10 / O T 17	Proper 17
Proper 13 / Pent 11 / O T 18	Proper 18
Proper 14 / Pent 12 / O T 19	Proper 19
Proper 15 / Pent 13 / O T 20	Proper 20
Proper 16 / Pent 14 / O T 21	Proper 21
Proper 17 / Pent 15 / O T 22	Proper 22
Proper 18 / Pent 16 / O T 23	Proper 23
Proper 19 / Pent 17 / O T 24	Proper 24
Proper 20 / Pent 18 / O T 25	Proper 25
Proper 21 / Pent 19 / O T 26	Proper 26
Proper 22 / Pent 20 / O T 27	Proper 27
Proper 23 / Pent 21 / O T 28	Proper 28
Proper 24 / Pent 22 / O T 29	Proper 29
Proper 25 / Pent 23 / O T 30	Proper 30
Proper 26 / Pent 24 / O T 31	Proper 31
Proper 27 / Pent 25 / O T 32	Proper 32
Proper 28 / Pent 26 / O T 33	Proper 33
Christ The King (Proper 29 / O T 34)	Proper 34 / Christ The King / Reign Of Christ
Reformation Day (October 31)	Reformation Day (October 31)
All Saints' Day (November 1 or 1st Sunday in November)	All Saints' Day (November 1)
Thanksgiving Day (4th Thursday of November)	Thanksgiving Day (2nd Monday of October)

*O T = Ordinary Time

www.ingramcontent.com/pod-product-compliance
Lightning Source LLC
Chambersburg PA
CBHW060133050426
42448CB00010B/2108